POWER AND POLICY

America's Role in World Affairs

SENATOR CLAIBORNE PELL

POWER AND POLICY
America's Role in World Affairs

W · W · NORTON & COMPANY · INC · *New York*

First Edition

ALL RIGHTS RESERVED
Published simultaneously in Canada
by George J. McLeod Limited, Toronto

Library of Congress Cataloging in Publication Data

Pell, Claiborne, 1918–
  Power and policy.

  1. U.S.—Foreign relations—1945–   I. Title.
E744.P34   327.73   75-39581
ISBN 0-393-05223-0

PRINTED IN THE UNITED STATES OF AMERICA

1 2 3 4 5 6 7 8 9 0

To Nuala, with infinite love.

Contents

Preface

As a member of the Senate and its Foreign Relations Committee, and as a former career diplomat, I have a long-standing interest in the foreign affairs of our country. I have devoted much of my time in public life to this enormously complex problem—to the point where some of my Rhode Island constituents have voiced criticism.

The truth is that my interest in the welfare of my constituents and of my country is at the heart of concern for the course —or perhaps I should say, the drift—of U.S. foreign policy.

During the Second World War there was a story about a well-dressed gentleman in London, at the height of the German air raids, being challenged by a group of military officers. They demanded to know why a young, able-bodied man like himself was not in uniform in such a time.

"The reason I'm not in uniform," he told them, "is because I'm with the Foreign Office. And if it hadn't been for the Foreign Office, you wouldn't *have* your bloody war!"

Few people, unfortunately, are interested in the intricacies of foreign policy. But everyone suffers in the wars that result when foreign policy fails, including the people of my own state of Rhode Island.

It is that thought which has moved me to make whatever contributions I could to the foreign policy of the country I am privileged to serve—and to write this book.

Acknowledgment

In the writing of this book, I pay immense tribute to Will Sparks. The depth and breadth of his knowledge, his ability as a writer, and his vast experience have all been put to full use in its preparation.

It has often been said that it is easy to make a simple thought a complicated one, but it is a very difficult job to make a complicated one simple. But this, to make the complicated a bit simpler, has been the thrust of this little primer on foreign relations.

I also thank immensely Cathryn Krupa for all her time and patient work in typing and proofreading this manuscript.

POWER AND POLICY

America's Role in World Affairs

CHAPTER ONE

What Are the Lessons
of History?

"Those who cannot remember the past," said the philosopher Santayana, "are condemned to repeat it."

The truth of that statement has applied so obviously to so many of the events of recent decades that to quote it today is almost to recite a cliché. Yet its central wisdom remains and we ignore it at our peril. Moreover, nowhere do the lessons of history seem more frequently forgotten than in the conduct of American foreign policy.

A nation's foreign policy consists both of the objectives which it seeks in relation to other countries, and also of the means by which it pursues those goals. The first goal of any nation's policies is, of course, national survival—with the prospect of war as a last line of defense always a tacit possibility. But national interests extend beyond mere survival. Foreign policies have been devised—and wars have been fought—to enlarge territories, increase trade or protect overseas investments, and even to propagate the faith, whether that faith be Judaism, Christianity, Mohammedanism, the *liberté, égalité, et fraternité* which Napoleon's armies carried on their banners to most of Western Europe, or modern communism and fascism.

None of this is to say that international relations need always be unfriendly or foreign policies aggressive. For there is such a thing as enlightened self-interest which recognizes that the welfare of our own country is often dependent upon the welfare of others; it is from such recognition that we get lowering of trade barriers, arms limitations, international guarantees of freedom on the high seas, and a host of other treaties and agreements in which each nation abandons some possible short-term advantage for the long-term good of all.

To the student of diplomacy, however, nothing seems clearer than this: every nation's foreign policy should be based on that nation's true interests, to the exclusion of sentiment, nostalgia, or evangelical fervor. Lord Palmerston, to my mind, best expressed this view when he said: "We have no eternal allies, and we have no perpetual enemies. Our interests are eternal and perpetual, and those interests it is our duty to follow." I believe strongly in the wisdom of that dictum and, further, that much of our past and present foreign policy errors may be traced directly to our tendency to disregard it, to follow policies rooted in tradition rather than in true national interest.

Or perhaps it would be more precise to say that, historically, national interests tend to change more quickly than do national policies. Let us take, for example, the policy which became known during the Second World War as the doctrine of unconditional surrender. It is an interesting example because of the historical parallel it affords between similar events separated in time by nearly two thousand years: Rome vs. Carthage, and the United States vs. Germany. Both are examples of policies inappropriate to the interests of the nation which formulated them, and also of the dangers of evangelical fervor in the formulation of basic policy.

The struggle between Rome and Carthage for control of the Mediterranean world lasted 118 years, from 264 to 146 B.C. It involved what we today would call three "hot" wars—the three Punic Wars—and an almost continuous "cold" war in between. From our viewpoint, the most instructive of those conflicts was the third and final hot war, which lasted from 148 to 146 B.C. and ended in the total, permanent destruction of Carthage. Instructive because, first, the war was unnecessary and, second, it was prolonged and intensified beyond all military necessity by Roman policy, which would be satisfied with nothing less than the complete erasure of Carthage. To cite a distinguished military authority, General Donald Armstrong in his book *The Reluctant Warriors:* "Rome did not need this war. Her security was assured by her great superiority in population and by her strong army and navy. Carthage, desiring only to preserve the peace, was no threat, actual or potential, to Rome. Nevertheless, Rome goaded Carthage, a nation of usually reluctant warriors, into becoming a raging enemy."

As the general goes on to point out, Rome violated a principle that no one has defined better than Rabelais:

> Sound military doctrine teaches us that you must never reduce your enemy to desperation, because such a plight multiplies his force and increases his courage which had already vanished. There is no better help for men who are demoralized and worn out by fatigue than to have no hope of salvation. How many victories have been taken out of the hands of the victorious by the vanquished when victors were not satisfied with reasonable achievements, but attempted total destruction of the enemy.

By the time Rome came to her ultimate confrontation with Carthage, she had already accomplished the purpose of the anti-Carthaginian policies which she had pursued over the previous century and through two wars.

Carthage had long ceased to be a threat to Roman hegemony in the Mediterranean. Her navy, once so much more powerful than Rome's, was now a small fleet of merchant vessels; her army, by Roman standards, inconsequential; Carthage had given hostages to Rome and agreed to an annual tribute, which was paid promptly and in full.

On the eve of the final conflict, seeking desperately to avoid new hostilities, the Carthaginians totally disarmed themselves —delivering to the Roman legions every sword, spear, and catapult in the city. Whereupon the Romans decreed that the Carthaginians should also abandon their capital city, move their women and children ten miles inland, and permit Carthage to be razed. Then, and only then, did the Carthaginians go to war. Helpless, disarmed, without allies, having nothing to lose, they managed to fight on for three years. And although they were defeated in the end, the cost to Rome in lives and treasure was incalculable—and wholly unnecessary because Rome's real interests were already secured before the fighting even began. Rome's policy, however, had not caught up with this fact, and so the ancient world got the Third Punic War.

I have stressed these two-thousand-year-old events because they teach a lesson which, whether or not we have learned it today, had demonstrably not been absorbed by our policy makers during the Second World War. Otherwise we should never have had the doctrine of unconditional surrender which, in the view of most authorities, unnecessarily prolonged the war by giving the Nazi leadership a new lease on life, helping them to convince the German people that they had nothing to lose. It was the Carthaginian error all over again. Let me briefly review the facts.

In January 1943, two months after the successful allied landings in North Africa, President Roosevelt and Prime Minister Churchill met at Casablanca. The primary purpose of the meeting was to plan the coming military campaigns in the Mediterranean. But in his press conference at the close of the meeting (January 26, 1943), President Roosevelt offered a remark which, most historians agree, cost the world incalculable, unnecessary losses of lives and resources.

Recalling the phrase, "unconditional surrender," used by

General Grant in the Civil War, FDR informed reporters that the Allies' war plans were "to compel the unconditional surrender of the Axis." As the respected military analyst of the *New York Times*, Hanson W. Baldwin, observed in his book, *Great Mistakes of the War,* there is little doubt that this unfortunate remark had the effect of stiffening enemy resistance and postponing the day of surrender in Germany and Japan, and possibly Italy as well.

Louis P. Lochner, the editor and translator of the wartime diaries of German propaganda minister Paul Joseph Goebbels, has written: "Goebbels . . . was convinced that a propaganda policy of the Allies, by which a differentiation was made between the Nazi regime and its crimes on the one hand and the decent element of Germany and its feeling for honor on the other, would have torn Germany asunder and caused great difficulties for the regime. The historian of the future will probably have to re-evaluate the wisdom of the Allied insistence upon unconditional surrender which was predicated on the assumption that all Germans were alike. Goebbels, after all, knew something about propaganda and the psychology of the German people."

Actually, Dr. Goebbels' expertise was unnecessary. The mistake had nothing to do with anything peculiar to Germany: it was Cato's famous rallying cry, "Delinda est Carthago," applied to the modern world—with predictable results.

It is important to note that the call for unconditional surrender was not simply an ill-considered remark by a president of the United States at a press conference. The phrase had been approved in advance by both Prime Minister Churchill and the British War Cabinet. It was, therefore, a statement of policy—and a policy at variance with the true interests of the policy makers.

More than one element entered into this blunder. In part, it was apparently intended to reassure our Russian allies that the British and the Americans intended to fight to the finish.

Another ingredient, in my opinion, was the passionate hatred which developed during the war against the Axis powers as the result of their atrocities and the crimes against humanity, especially those committed by the German forces. But outrage, fervor, hatred, revulsion—call it what you will—while frequently understandable and even praiseworthy is *never* alone a sound basis for formulating policy. Unless these passions, however justified, are rigorously excluded from exercising a prime role in policy decisions, the resulting policy is likely to be, at best, ineffective and, at worst, disastrous.

In the tumult of war, it is usually reason which is first to succumb and slowest to recover. So perhaps we might attribute the kind of error we've been discussing—both the Roman and our own—to the passions accompanying battle. Unfortunately for this somewhat comforting thesis, we have continued to formulate policy in much the same manner in the quarter-century since the Second World War ended.

Within a few years of the cessation of hostilities, our former allies, China and the USSR, had become our chief antagonists in what was to become known as the cold war, while we turned increasingly to our former enemies, Germany and Japan, in our search for stability in Europe and Asia—as perfect an illustration as one might wish for the truth of Palmerston's dictum that "we have no eternal allies, and we have no perpetual enemies." But what has been our policy? How did it evolve?

The inability of the Russians and the Western allies to agree on the postwar status of Germany, which became clear at the Moscow Conference of Foreign Ministers in 1947, ended hope for friendly cooperation between the Communist and non-Communist worlds. The United States reacted by launching our policy of containment, designed to hold Russia and her Communist satellites within existing boundaries until such time—and we were confident that the time would come —as the Communist "empire" should fall apart from internal strains and antagonisms.

The first major step in our containment policy came in March 1947 when President Truman asked the Congress for $400,000,000 in military and economic aid for Greece and Turkey—thus launching what became known as the Truman Doctrine. Its general principle, as stated by the president in making his request, was "that it must be the policy of the United States to support free peoples who are resisting attempted subjugation by armed minorities or by outside pressures." In the president's mind as he spoke was the guerrilla warfare then being waged against the royal government of Greece, aided by heavy infiltration from Greece's three Communist neighbors, and Russian pressure against Turkey to yield her traditional control of the Dardanelles. With Korea, and later with Vietnam, we were to realize the scope of that commitment and of the principle from which it sprang.

Along with our efforts to strengthen Greece and Turkey against the threat of armed aggression, the United States launched a massive campaign to stimulate the economic recovery of Europe on the sound theory that this was the best defense against the spread of communism into Western Europe. In announcing America's willingness to assist the economies of European nations, we should recall, Secretary of State George Marshall drew no distinction between Communist and non-Communist Europe. As originally announced (in June 1947), "Marshall Plan" aid was available to all. Moscow, however, denounced it as an "instrument of American imperialism" and several Eastern European countries, including Poland and Czechoslovakia—as well as Finland—were obliged against their will to decline the offer.

In fact, Czechoslovakia publicly moved to participate in this Marshall Plan until the Kremlin forced her to reverse herself. This was the final tragedy, the *coup de grâce,* for Jan Masaryk. As an American Foreign Service officer then stationed in Czechoslovakia, I believed—and continue to believe

—that this reversal played the largest single role in Masaryk's subsequent death, no matter whether self-inflicted or caused by Communist police agents. (Personally, I have come to the conclusion that his death was the result of assassination and not suicide.)

The third leg of the stool upon which we proposed to stand in our "contain communism" campaign was the "Point Four" program announced at the beginning of 1949. Just as the Marshall Plan was calculated to frustrate communism in Europe by alleviating poverty and unemployment, so this "bold new program for making the benefits of our scientific advances and industrial progress available for the improvement and growth of underdeveloped areas" (President Truman's words) was designed to strengthen the resistance of countries in Asia and Latin America by raising their standard of living.

It is not my purpose here to discuss the early successes or failures of these programs—although the successes far outweighed the failures in those years—but, rather, to stress one significant fact: Truman Doctrine, Marshall Plan, Point Four Program, and many accompanying actions were originally conceived as part of the containment policy, the purpose of which was to buy time for the non-Communist world while international communism slowly dissolved under the stress of its own internal contradictions.

Given this theory, it would obviously be to our advantage to encourage this erosion through trade, through cultural contacts, and bridge building of all possible varieties with individual communist countries. This is where our interest lay—and yet this is precisely what we did not do. Somehow—perhaps through listening to our own rhetoric—we became so obsessed with the dangers of aggressive, monolithic international communism that we forgot the origin and purpose of our own policy. Throughout the 1950s and 1960s, consequently, we missed one opportunity after another to encourage separatist movements within the Communist bloc and, indeed, actually helped to frustrate such developments.

Time moved on, but American policy stayed still.

Donald S. Zagoria, one of the government's leading analysts of Communist bloc politics during the decade of the fifties, has written of the holders of such views:

> It seems to me they mistakenly attribute to the Communist world a monolithism which, if it ever actually existed, clearly has not existed since the death of Stalin. Their preoccupation with what is undoubtedly the very real challenge of international Communism has prevented [them] . . . from crediting the evidence: first of Tito's break with Stalin, then of the discord between Gomulka and Khrushchev, and finally of the Sino-Soviet conflict. Their fear of a lowering in the Western guard has led them to deny the development of pluralism in the world Communist movement and prevented them, I believe, from making the sound assessment of the strengths and weaknesses of that movement which is essential to maintenance of the Western guard.

Like Santayana's fanatic, having forgotten our purpose, we just redoubled our efforts.

WAR AND PEACE

If the first lesson of history is that foreign policy should be —but often is not—based on true and ever-changing national interests, the second important lesson is this: wars, big or little, are at least as natural to man as peace, but they are not inevitable.

When we consider that there has been, conservatively, at least one war raging somewhere in the world every thirty years, it is difficult to maintain that peace is man's natural condition. Any study of diplomatic history, moreover, reconfirms the accuracy of Clausewitz's observation that war is merely the pursuit of policy by other means.

The fact that war is natural does not, however, mean that it is inevitable. Conflicts between nations can be cooled down or contained. Historical examples of success in such endeavors are obviously harder to find than examples of our failures. In part, perhaps, because they are rarer but also because the event that does not happen—the war that never was—is difficult to trace.

One clear instance from our own history was the series of peaceful settlements with England of disputes over the American northeastern frontier following the War of 1812. Ill feeling and a long series of crises continued between the two countries for decades after the war, but renewed warfare was successfully avoided until ultimately arbitration became a habit.

One of the chief features of the 1812 war had been naval engagements on Lake Erie and Lake Ontario, and a naval armaments race on Lake Ontario. Yet in 1816, our ambassador to England, John Quincy Adams, was able to persuade the British government to accept a freeze on naval armament in the Great Lakes. This agreement, which led to what is usually known as the Rush-Bagot Treaty, was not the result of friendship or good feeling. Adams was able to demonstrate to the British that, whatever initial advantage they might gain, American superiority in population and resources in the region would make us the ultimate victors in a protracted naval armament race—and hence a voluntary limitation on that race was sound policy for England.

The Rush-Bagot agreement, ratified by the Senate in 1818, is often cited as the beginning of the unguarded frontier between the United States and Canada. In fact, no longer needed as a fort, Fort Ticonderoga, on the neck joining Lakes Champlain and George, was acquired by my great great grandfather, William F. Pell, as a summer place, and has been used for peaceful and museum purposes by my family ever since. Tension continued, however, between our two countries for more than fifty years. During the Civil War, the United States gave notice of (and later withdrew) its intention to terminate the treaty. Land fortifications north of Fort Ticonderoga were maintained and regularly reinforced during crises in Anglo-American relations—which were frequent and could have easily led to a renewal of the hostilities of 1812.

Yet the Rush-Bagot agreement, the ultimate demilitarization of the frontier and numerous other devices for cooling down Anglo-American relations were successfully carried out—usually through one form or another of a mutually accepted arbitration commission. It is an excellent example of what can be accomplished when policy, although unable at once to eliminate causes of friction between two nations, is directed toward at least containing them and cooling down the animosities associated with them.

We should not overlook, in reviewing these peaceful settlements, the important role of public opinion. For this was also the beginning of the era of the peace movement. Largely as a reaction to the Napoleonic Wars and especially the War of 1812, there sprang up in both Europe and America organized societies whose aim was to lobby for peace, and who believed, with Benjamin Franklin, that "There never was a good war or a bad peace." Federalist opponents of the 1812 war organized themselves under the banner, "Friends of Peace," and in 1815, the year the war ended, peace societies were formed in both New York and Massachusetts. The largest and longest-lived of these groups, the American Peace Society, was formed in 1828, and by 1861 there were at least fifty local peace societies throughout the United States. Similar groups were formed in England, and between 1848 and 1851 international peace congresses were held in Brussels, Paris, Frankfort, and London.

Members of these societies lobbied in Congress against large military expenditures and with governments here and in Europe for such causes as arms reductions, prohibition of munitions sales to belligerents, and courts of arbitration.

Their effectiveness is hard to measure, but they served to make governments aware of the widespread sentiment for peace and, while they didn't prevent the spread of nineteenth century imperialism, they were a definite influence on the "cooling down" of conflict which characterizes this period in our history. Many of our immigrants of those years came from war-torn Europe to avoid the forced military service or draft then in effect in so many countries on that quarrelsome continent. They were in a position to appreciate, as General Omar Bradley was later to observe, that "for every man in whom war has inspired sacrifice, courage and love, there are many more whom it has degraded with brutality, callousness, and greed."

The popular peace movement of the nineteenth century deserves more attention than historians generally give to it. Had there been more awareness, I suspect that many of our recent and present leaders would have been less prone to dismiss the early anti-Vietnam demonstrators as irrelevant and inconsequential. Peace movements are as American as apple pie and they have, on more than one occasion, profoundly influenced national policy.

AGREEMENTS TO DISAGREE

A third major lesson of diplomatic history, obvious to even the most casual student, is that international agreements are honored only so long as each participant considers it in his national interests to do so; in other words, so long as the costs of violating the agreement exceed whatever benefits might be expected from the violation.

Americans are prone to think of treaty violations as a form of nefarious activity indulged in by foreigners, especially the Hitlers, Stalins, and Maos, about which we are entitled to be righteously indignant. We can maintain this conviction, however, only through a continuing collective amnesia when it comes to our own history.

My own Indian ancestors learned, through a long series of tragic injustices which continue to this day, that the white man's treaties were literally not worth the paper on which they were written. While the European settlers were a thin sprinkling of strangers in a strange land, nothing was more desirable than a treaty of peace with "the noble red man"; when the western migration reached torrential proportions and white settlers needed land, the maxim quickly developed that "the only good Indian is a dead Indian." This was almost explicitly spelled out in what must surely be one of the more disgraceful documents in American history—President Chester A. Arthur's First Annual Message to the Congress in 1881:

> It was natural, at a time when the national territory seemed almost illimitable and contained many millions of acres far outside the bounds of civilized settlements, that a policy should have been initiated which more than aught else has been the fruitful source of our Indian complications.

> I refer, of course, to the policy of dealing with the various Indian tribes as separate nationalities, or relegating them by treaty stipulations to the occupancy of immense reservations in the West, and of encouraging them to live a savage life, undisturbed by any earnest and well-directed efforts to bring them under the influences of civilization.

> The unsatisfactory results which have sprung from this policy are becoming apparent to all.

> As the white settlements have crowded the borders of the reservations, the Indians, sometimes contentedly and sometimes against their will, have been transferred to other hunting grounds, from which they have again been dislodged whenever their new found homes have been desired by the adventurous settlers.

These removals and the frontier collisions by which they have often been preceded have led to frequent and disastrous conflicts between the races.

It is profitless to discuss here which of them has been chiefly responsible for the disturbances whose recital occupies so large a space upon the pages of our history.

The Indian appealed in vain to the sanctity of his hundreds of treaties with the Great White Father in Washington—treaties typically assuring him rights to his lands "while the sun shall rise and the moon continues to shine." The settlers needed land and if they were to be obliged to fight a few Indian "wars" (more often massacres), so be it; the benefits were so much greater than the costs that the nation could easily afford to pay them.

Our European friends also discovered very early in our history that, in adhering to treaties, Americans did not greatly differ from the rest of mankind. The Treaty of Alliance with France (1778), so indispensable to the success of the American Revolution, had become by 1793 an entangling alliance. A companion treaty from the year 1778 assured privileged treatment for French naval vessels in American ports—but when France appealed for those rights fifteen years later, they were not only refused, but the Congress soon formally abrogated the treaty.

I cite these examples with no sense either of moral approbation or moral disapprobation. My personal view is that our country has, over most of our short history, been relatively trustworthy in its international relations. We have been usually sincere at the time we made our commitments, and we have tried to honor those commitments to a degree unusual among nations—more than once to our own national disadvantage. But the law of history which says that nations generally honor treaties in proportion to their potential gain vs. loss holds true of ourselves as well as others, and everyone—

including ourselves—will function better in this imperfect world if we try to remember it.

We must bear in mind that the action of violating a treaty is always costly in itself; it cheapens the reputation of the nation involved and cheapens the value of that nation's commitments. Thus, the cost must be cranked into the equation when a nation weighs its alternative courses of action.

Moreover, the more ironclad the treaty provisions and the more built-in sanctions it contains and the more people who are party to a treaty's provisions, the more costly becomes the violation of that treaty. This last, incidentally, is a reason why secret treaties are to be avoided.

It is also true that negotiations in order to be successful must be conducted from positions of equal strength. Otherwise, if one nation is much stronger than the other, the agreement that is arrived upon may well not last since it is an imposed agreement and, when the second nation becomes more equal in power, it will seek to reverse the earlier settlement. An excellent example of that was the Versailles Treaty which sought to impose a settlement on Germany which simply didn't survive.

It has taken me a while to arrive at this thought. In fact, when I first ran for office I used the phrase "We must only negotiate from strength." But the longer I have been in the Senate, the more convinced I have become that negotiations will result in far more lasting settlements if they are conducted by equals rather than one strong and one weak party. In this regard, I well remember a conversation Senator Albert Gore and I had with Premier Alexei Kosygin in Moscow in November of 1968. Kosygin emphasized the thought that, for our arms limitations talks to be effective, they must be conducted from positions of reasonably similar strength. And President Nixon, upon assuming office, changed his position from the campaign oratory of advocating a position of only negotiating from strength to one of negotiating from a position of sufficiency. I believe the word *sufficiency* in this regard is an excellent one and that President Nixon should be commended for it and for this change.

All men are human, no men are beasts, all men are equally children of God. This article of faith for all who believe in the brotherhood of man is a good basis for any foreign policy. It does not mean that men are saints. What it does mean is that we should not waste our time looking for villains and heroes—or that, at least, we should not use our subjective decisions about the good guys or the bad guys as a basis for national policy. This must be done on a clear-eyed analysis of national self-interest. As Winston Churchill said in explaining England's wartime alliance with the Soviet Union, "I would make a deal with the Devil himself if it would defeat Hitler."

WHY WE FIGHT

Man's nature—his needs and desires—remain constant. They are the common thread which runs through international relations from ancient Greece to modern Asia. Once he has organized himself into a definable group—whether it be tribe, city-state, or nation-state—man will expect his leaders to protect his life and his property. He will expect his leaders to maximize his advantages, sometimes aggressively at the expense of his neighbors, where the cost seems acceptable. His leaders, in turn, will sometimes use foreign adventures to strengthen their position at home; history is filled, for example, with instances of wars which had their origin in some leader's desire to blame foreigners for his own obvious failure to deliver on the promises he had made to his own people.

As a general rule, we may say that in international relations, while men do not precisely live in a state of nature, neither are they angels. We can generally expect any political entity, from the largest to the smallest, to seize whatever opportunities it believes itself to have to increase either its security or its prosperity. The techniques change, but the basic drives and goals are eternal. Or at least have been to date, and it would be utopian to assume that they will change greatly in the foreseeable future.

In past eras, distance was a great bulwark to the freedom and independence of nations. The Mongols and their ancestors were often at war with their Eurasian neighbors, and these same neighbors, driven westward, made war on—and ultimately destroyed—the Roman empire. But Mongol did not fight Roman, although both were warlike, because they were separated by vast spaces, and there was a limit even to the prowess of the famous Mongol cavalry and the efficiency of the vaunted Roman highways.

Because of modern technology, virtually all of these barriers have crumbled. One hundred and fifty years ago, a British ambassador to Rome, recalled by his government, would have taken almost as long to get from Rome to London as it took Julius Caesar almost two thousand years earlier. All our great advances in transportation and communications have been made in little more than a century, and there are many still alive who were on earth before man first found wings at Kittyhawk.

Even more significant than the extraordinary explosion of technology during the last century or so is the rate of technological change which confronts us today. Everyone is familiar with the observation that 90 percent of all the scientists who ever lived are alive and working today. We often tend, however, to overlook the concrete consequences of this fact. From the Wright Brothers first flight at Kittyhawk, North Carolina, to Lindbergh's crossing of the Atlantic, there elapsed only some twenty years. From Lindbergh's flight to the atomic bomb was approximately another twenty years. And in the year in which Lindbergh made his historic flight, Dr. Robert Goddard was performing the first small experiments with his rockets that would, within Charles Lindbergh's own lifetime, place men on the moon. Today scientists tell us that every seven years sees a complete revolution in computer technology, and that by the year 2000, given this rate of development, the computer will almost certainly be a true rival to the human intelligence.

In the following pages I propose to examine, in the light of the previous observations, what I believe will be the principal challenges to American foreign policy in the decade ahead, and what should be—not so much our policies themselves—as the philosophical and political bases for arriving at sound, prudent decisions as we try to cope with the world around us.

CHAPTER TWO

What Does America Want?

It would seem to be a fairly obvious fact that we are more likely to arrive at our destination if, at the start of the journey, we have in mind some specific destination, or at least a clear idea of the direction we intend to travel. Yet a lack of specific goals, or even a firm compass heading by which we intend to steer the ship of state, has all too often been the chief characteristic of American foreign "policy." The obvious lack of clearly defined objectives has long been the U.S. trademark in international affairs.

A certain amount of ambiguity—at least publicly—is necessary and probably unavoidable in the pursuit of diplomacy. A broad range of possibilities for agreement is the ideal arsenal which the professional diplomat brings to international negotiations. Somewhere in his briefcase there is—or should be—a memorandum outlining his government's minimum acceptable position. And this is—or should be—a top secret document; in the hands of the other side it would destroy the negotiation before it began. The diplomat, like the poker player, needs a few hole cards kept firmly face-down on the table to keep the other players guessing.

There is a difference, however, between mystifying the other players and not knowing what's in one's own hand.

Egypt's late president, Abdel Nasser, once remarked to an American representative that "the genius of you Americans is that you never make clear-cut, simple stupid mistakes; you only make complicated stupid mistakes—which makes us work at the possibility that there may be something we are overlooking."

He may have given us too much credit. The real difficulty with American foreign policy is that it too often resembles a dromedary in the joke which says that "a camel is a horse designed by a committee."

Foreign policy cannot be designed by a committee—and here I include the Senate Foreign Relations Committee, on which I have had the privilege of serving for many years. We on the committee can, as we did at the time of our original Vietnam hearings, lay the groundwork for our change of policy in Vietnam which in turn influenced President Johnson's decision not to run for a second term. We can launch new concepts and policies for our nation to follow, as I sought to do when I first introduced my Ocean Space Treaty. Or, we can, with due regard for the necessary secrets of state, try to make sure that the people are kept informed about their government's activities in the international community; we can recommend—or refuse to recommend—treaties proposed by the president. But we cannot and should not formulate the details of our nation's foreign policy. This must be done by the president, with the assistance of his State Department, National Security Council, and all the other agencies of the executive branch.

Foreign policy, any more than a horse, cannot be successfully designed by a committee. It must be determined by the president who holds office at the mandate of the majority of the people and is answerable to them for all of his policies, including foreign policy. It is the president who can best spell out for the world and our own people the principal objectives of our foreign policy. I might add that in my years on the Foreign Relations Committee I have never known a member to deny that proposition. The Congress and its committees are much like the board of directors of a business corporation.

The board is the governing body of the company but it does not spell out the details of policy formation. This is, rather, the responsibility of the chief executive officer—which in our country's case is the president of the United States.

In the mind of every national leader there must exist, like so many lighthouses, certain goals or objectives which in his best judgment represent his country's best interests in the international arena. These goals will vary with the times and the man, based on his own experience and philosophy and how he relates them to the current environment. This will always be a major constituent of national foreign policy, although it may not be recognized as such.

Foreign policy cannot be programmed by a computer; leadership is essential—and the nature of the leader makes a large difference. Hitler's, Stalin's, and Churchill's utterly conflicting views of Europe have had profound effects on the course of history during our lifetime. Powerful leaders have, of course, created much harm and suffering when misguided policies are pursued. But this is not the only danger.

One of the greatest dangers is encountered when a leader has no particular philosophy or underlying principle but is, instead, mainly interested in his own political survival. When this condition becomes manifest in a political leader, he should be cast aside. And one of the advantages of a democratic society is that this can be done quickly and without revolution.

Actually, it is rare even in totalitarian societies that a man becomes a political leader unless he has a concern for the general well-being of his country and compatriots. But this is a quality which can be and often is corrupted by the habit of power and the stultification of time. In a democracy, this condition tends to be self-correcting: the leader who by his actions loses the confidence of his people ceases to be a leader. This is the principal reason why, as Winston Churchill once observed, that while democracy is a terribly inefficient form of government, we are obliged to say for it that all the other forms are worse.

Even in democracies, however, changes of leadership take time and it is in these periods of time when political leaders are guided by motives of personal survival rather than a basic philosophy or vision that the nation they lead may well lose its dynamism. "Where there is no vision," we are told in the Book of Proverbs, "the people perish." The phenomenon is not new.

It might be argued, of course, that if all national leaders were strong, determined men with inflexible objectives, the possibilities of world clash and destruction would be greatly increased. A study of history plainly shows, however, that wars are far more often caused by drift, indecision, and miscalculation than by head-on conflicts between two opposing philosophies.

Recounting the outbreak of the Spanish American War, for example, the historian Samuel Eliot Morison cites the crucial role of President McKinley—whom he describes as "a kindly soul in a spineless body." Following the sinking of the *U.S.S. Maine* in Havana harbor, he observes, "The American minister at Madrid cabled Washington that if nothing were done to humiliate Spain he could obtain a settlement of the Cuban question on the basis of autonomy, independence, or even cession to the United States. He believed that Sagasta [the Spanish premier] was ready to accord Cuba the same freedom as Britain had to Canada.

"Any president with a backbone would have seized this opportunity for an honorable solution. McKinley, a veteran of 1861, did not want war. . . . Wall Street, big business, and a majority of the Republican senators backed him up. . . . But Congress and the press, and 'Young Republicans' like Henry Cabot Lodge, were clamoring for war, and McKinley became obsessed with the notion that if he did not give way, the Republican Party would be broken. After much prayer and hesitation, he decided to yield. A year later he confessed, 'But for the inflamed state of public opinion, and the fact that Congress could no longer be held in check, a peaceful solution might have been had.' "

Events of recent years have left many convinced that unnecessary conflict and violence have resulted from the failure of strong-minded leaders to heed the advice of Congress and the true desires of the people; this should not be allowed to obscure the fact that the same catastrophic consequences can and do result from the failure by weak leaders to resist the tides of transient passion in conflicts between nations. What counts is courageous leadership, guided by deep insight and conviction concerning the true aspirations and interest of the people. Without this, all else is futile. The strong-willed leader following wrong policies and the weak leader following no policy at all are equally dangerous.

THERE ARE LIMITS TO EVERYTHING

Specific goals or objectives, even under the wisest and most forceful leadership, will not, however, enable us to achieve our national purposes if those objectives exceed our capacities. And by "capacity" I mean not what a nation can achieve when stretched all out, but what it can produce without a wrenching dislocation of the people's normal way of life. During World War II the United States, by devoting 45 percent of its gross national product to the conduct of the war, performed miracles of production, troop deployment, and logistical supply operations around the world. We have the potential to do it again, if necessary. But to assume that this potential is synonymous with our capacity, and base our foreign policy goals on that assumption, is to condemn ourselves to living in perpetual garrison state. And that is not the American way of life we set out to defend.

Germany's Propaganda Minister, Dr. Paul Joseph Goebbels, once said "The great strength of National Socialism is that we force our enemies to imitate us." I cannot accept that.

It is true, of course, that a far-seeing leader will sometimes deliberately choose an objective for the precise purpose of developing or stretching a nation's capacity. All too frequently the objective has entailed violent conflict, as when Bismark used the Franco-Prussian War to forge a loose confederation of Germanic states into the modern German nation. But there are also economic goals which can be set. Stalin did this with his five-year plans and—at a terrible cost in human suffering and starvation—did in fact succeed in stretching the capacity of the Russian people.

Questions of morality or humaneness aside, Stalin largely succeeded because his goals, though ruthlessly pursued, were essentially obtainable. In contrast, Mao Tse-tung, with a similar philosophy and equal ruthlessness, launched the Great Leap Forward—and failed. He failed because the goals set were simply beyond all possibility of attainment; as a result, as in any effort where a nation's reach exceeds its ability to grasp, China found itself worse-off than when it started. Subsequently, with more modest goals and pragmatic methods, far more was accomplished.

To put it all in a simple statement: For a nation's foreign policy to succeed, there must be firm leadership pursuing specific objectives, and these objectives must be reasonably obtainable.

When leadership is weak, or the goals vague, or the objectives unreasonable—any nation is flirting with disaster. The United States is not exempt from this law of political nature. By disregarding it on many occasions in the past, we have suffered greatly as a people and will do so in the future—unless we face up firmly to the international challenges which confront us as a nation and determine with clarity what we, history's largest, wealthiest, and most powerful democracy, do and do not wish to do in the world arena.

THE INADEQUACY OF IDEOLOGY

By urging the need for strong leadership based upon an underlying philosophy seeking reasonably specific goals, I am not arguing for an ideological approach to foreign policy. Quite the opposite. I believe, in fact, that the ideologists of history have been responsible for at least as much unnecessary conflict and suffering as the demagogues, and perhaps more. Their evangelical fervor often causes them to lose sight of reasonable balance between means and ends—a prominent factor in the conduct of Russian foreign policy in the 1920s and '30s, and in U.S. policy during the 1950s and '60s, particularly in the latter decade, with regard to Vietnam. Until recently, at least, this has also been true of Communist China; indeed, one of the most hopeful signs for peace in the world is that China's high ranking ideologists are gradually either becoming more pragmatic or are being replaced by more pragmatic leaders.

In addition to his tendency to lose sight of ends and means, the ideologist also has a dangerous habit of blinding himself to reality. He attempts to twist the facts until they meet his own standards of how events should be happening. Prior to U.S. entry into the Second World War, for example, German intelligence agents sent many reports to Berlin about America's potential capacity for armament production, mobilization, and so forth. Senior officials in Berlin, however, greeted the estimates with disbelief. Locked in the Nazi ideology which decreed that all democracies must be by nature decadent and inefficient, they began to accuse their agents of being pro-American. The agents, in turn, began to tone down their estimates of American capabilities—which protected themselves, and satisfied the Nazi ideologists, but also caused the German war effort to be based on less and less reliable intelligence estimates. There are many who believe that a similar phenomenon afflicted U.S. policy towards China when State Department "China experts" during the McCarthy era suffered adverse personal consequences for predicting—correctly, as it turned out—that Mao Tse-tung would probably prevail in mainland China. Their professional evaluations were ignored, punished, and, one suspects, in many cases, toned down to avoid the wrath of the ideologists of dedicated anti-Communism.

Ideology, like sentimentality, can be extremely harmful in relations among nations.

Woodrow Wilson is the outstanding example of our American tendency to engage in what has been characterized as missionary diplomacy. President Wilson was guided in his foreign policy decisions not merely by a desire to pursue the national interests of the United States, but also by a sincere wish to use American power to improve the conditions of people throughout the world. A virtuous and sincere man, he nevertheless left the world with several examples of the harm which can result from free-floating idealism unaccompanied by a true conception of national purposes and capabilities. This is most clearly illustrated, perhaps, by his involvement with Mexico.

In 1911, a liberal coalition overthrew the corrupt dictatorship of Porfirio Díaz and installed Francisco Madero as president of Mexico. A month before President Wilson's inauguration, however, one of Madero's generals, Victoriano Huerta, assassinated his former leader and seized power. This represented a return of the reactionary old regime, but, since it promised stability, most of the great powers who had economic interests in Mexico quickly recognized Huerta's government. The American ambassador in Mexico also advised recognition. President Wilson refused, stating that, "I will not recognize a government of butchers." In so stating he was departing from an ancient tradition in the history of nations, that the question of recognition revolves around whether a particular government does or does not have a de facto control of the territory which it claims to represent, regardless of the methods by which it came to power. The introduction of morality judgments about the legitimacy of a particular regime is a fairly typical American diplomatic variation which would eventually, when the question of recognizing Communist China arose in the mid-twentieth century, confuse American relations with the nearly one-fourth of the human race which resides in mainland China.

President Wilson brought every possible pressure to bear on the Huerta regime. Although he did succeed in forcing the British to withdraw their recognition, he accomplished little else. When a small party of American sailors was arrested in the Port of Tampico in April 1914, President Wilson seized upon the affair as a case for sending American troops into Mexico. His only purpose, he told a reporter, was, "to help the people to secure their liberty." The actual intervention took place at Vera Cruz, where the Mexicans resisted fiercely, retreating only after the loss of several hundred men. The effect, to President Wilson's great surprise, was to unite the Mexican people to the point where the leader of the anti-Huerta armies vigorously denounced the Americans. President Wilson suddenly found himself engaged in a war in Mexico which he had strongly opposed. He was doing exactly what the critics of his own policies had always wanted him to do and was being deluged with protests by peace groups—his former supporters—from all over the United States. As the intricacies of the Mexican situation increased, the president ultimately found himself sending General Pershing and his troops across the Mexican border in pursuit of Pancho Villa in reprisal against unprovoked attacks against Americans in Northern Mexico and New Mexico. Villa, who was only a bandit, drew Pershing's forces deeper and deeper into Mexico, so alarming the Mexican government that there were several clashes between Pershing's forces and the Mexican regulars, and in June 1916 war between Mexico and the United States seemed almost inevitable. But, of course, by then the threat of war in Europe was becoming imminent and largely for this reason, early in 1917, President Wilson quietly recalled General Pershing's forces to American soil.

What moral can we read in this? An idealistic president, dedicated to the ideals of democracy and self-determination, uses American power to intervene in the internal affairs of a smaller country. Far from being hailed as an act of democratic generosity the intervention serves to unite the rebellious forces with their own dictatorial government. The American president finds himself in the end doing precisely what he has himself always opposed—using superior force to inflict America's will on a smaller power—and even then fails to accomplish his objective. This was not the first instance of such an event in America's history. Nor, unfortunately, was it the last.

At the end of World War I, Woodrow Wilson considered perhaps the most important of his Fourteen Points to be the principle of self-determination of a people. Yet, fifty years later, we find this principle being applied very selectively. We believe in self-determination for South Vietnam. We continue to make public obeisence towards it in the countries of Eastern Europe. Yet, we strongly oppose it in Formosa or East Pakistan.

SPAIN AND VIETNAM

Historical analogies are notoriously dangerous; it is all too easy to see similarities between historical events which were in fact quite different. But while history never precisely duplicates itself, there are always certain parallels which are instructive, if properly interpreted. I believe that there exists such a parallel between U.S. involvement in the war with Spain and in Vietnam. Also, that both involvements further illustrate the moral to be drawn from the Mexican adventures of President Wilson.

The war between Spain and the United States is also an excellent example of the complex interaction among the forces of idealism, national self-interest, domestic politics, and sheer historical happenstance which ultimately determines the fate of nations—and makes a truly rational foreign policy so difficult, if not impossible, to conduct.

From the viewpoint of national self-interest, the United States was concerned with Cuba as far back as the John Quincy Adams administration. Indeed, many historians believe that only the northerners who opposed acquisition of more slave territory prevented us from occupying Cuba well before the American Civil War (slavery was not abolished in Cuba until 1886).

The war with Spain, when it finally came, had little to do with economic interests or the doctrine of manifest destiny of a few years earlier. As we have already observed, the business community and the Establishment of President McKinley's own party were prepared to support him fully in efforts to avoid the conflict—had he chosen to make the effort. Unlike the war in Vietnam, the war with Spain was enormously popular with the American people.

The principal reason for that popularity was a growing knowledge, thanks to the yellow press, and, particularly, the newspapers of William Randolph Hearst, of the atrocities being perpetrated by Spain against the Cuban people. Those atrocities were real. It was here, in fact, that the Spanish governor of Cuba, General Valeriano Weyler, invented the technique of leading the rural population into "reconcentration" camps in order to deprive the anti-Spanish guerrillas of food and recruits. Conditions in the camps were wretched, death and disease were common, and the effect was to harden resistance, make the conflict cruel and bloody—and arouse the sympathetic passions of the American people. (A few generations later, the South Vietnamese were to adopt precisely the same ineffective technique with their fortified hamlet program in Vietnam—this time with the support of the American Government but with a similar effect on U.S. public opinion as the facts became known.)

The American government by no means endorsed the rebel position in Cuba. Although President McKinley, who was not a rich man, privately contributed $5,000 to the Red Cross Cuban relief fund, officially he urged, as in his message to Congress in December 1897, that Spain be given "a reasonable chance to realize her expectations" in the island. By the time the battleship *Maine* was blown up in Havana harbor, however, the public clamor for American intervention was so great that events were largely out of the government's control. When the president submitted a restrained report on the incident to the Congress, he was informed that if he continued to refuse to act, the Congress would probably declare war on its own. And so the United States went to war with Spain, by a joint resolution of the Congress which specifically disclaimed any intention of adding Cuban territory to the United States. This was a war fueled by the best instincts of the American people: compassion for the victims of tyranny and a conviction that, as children of the American Revolution, we had a moral obligation to the victims of foreign domination everywhere, and especially in our own hemisphere. That this led directly to our own colonization of the Philippines is one of the many ironies of history giving credence to the notion that the cobblestones of Hell consist mainly of good intentions, especially in foreign policy. But colonization was not the motive force behind our Cuban intervention.

How does this relate to Vietnam? While the Spanish-American War was one of the most popular wars in our history, the Vietnam war is undoubtedly the most unpopular. In the former, we see an administration moving reluctantly toward hostilities under the thrust of mounting public outrage and enthusiasm; in the latter we see a government moving reluctantly toward hostilities certain to be unpopular, but which it felt obliged to risk—*if we were to carry out our historic opposition to the forces of tyranny and oppression.*

The element common to these two military adventures is a misplaced idealism—hard as that concept may be to accept by those who persist in pursuing a devil theory of history. Neither the Cuban intervention nor the Vietnam intervention resulted from the desire for increased American domination of the Caribbean or Southeast Asia. One arose from a popular passion to liberate an afflicted people; the other from a cold calculation by government officials that freedom is indivisible and that if we permit totalitarian aggression to succeed anywhere in the world, we will ultimately succumb ourselves. In fighting Spain over Cuba, the American public was still fighting King George III; in fighting Ho Chi Minh, the American government was still fighting Adolph Hitler. Both excellent examples, incidentally, of why historical analogies can be so dangerous.

Yet I believe it true that neither the Spanish nor the Vietnamese conflicts were necessary to our national interests, nor would either have occurred had we based our policy on those true interests, to the exclusion of "sentiment, nostalgia, or evangelical fervor." This is a viewpoint often difficult to defend in national debates over foreign policy in specific instances—somewhat like coming out against motherhood or pursuing a cynical Machiavellian philosophy. It is, nevertheless, an inevitable conclusion for one who troubles to compare the costs in blood and treasure of pursuing the course of genuine, purely selfish national interests on the one hand, and altruism or evangelism on the other.

A *policy*, according to Webster, consists of "the principles on which any measure or course of action is based, having regard to both the ends arrived at and the means used to arrive at them." Every nation has foreign relations. This does not automatically imply that every nation has a foreign policy. Action and reaction in the world arena may result from a variety of causes, including internal political pressures, error, and blind chance. So the first question to be asked concerning the foreign affairs of any nation is whether its actions are, in fact, really based on some set of principles "having regard to both the ends arrived at and the means used to arrive at them."

Since the Second World War, the international posture of the United States has run the gamut from official indifference, through diplomatic and economic pressures, to armed intervention. We have sent Marines into Lebanon and the Dominican Republic, but not Cuba; we have fought violent wars in behalf of South Korea and South Vietnam, but declared a hands-off policy toward repression in Hungary and Czechoslovakia. A similar analysis might be made of the activities of the USSR, China, France, Egypt, and the other major players in the world arena. It is hard to find a common denominator for all these actions, or refusals to act.

The problems, and the dangers to peace, arise chiefly where a nation attempts to shape foreign policy for reasons other than national self-interest, or where it misconceives what its own interests are. All men desire the good, Plato tells us, but are often mistaken in their judgment of where the good is to be found.

> History, both recent and ancient, suggests the following corollaries:
> Foreign policy must be determined *only* by present and future national interests;
> Aggression is natural to man and he will readily resort to violence when he believes it significantly to his advantage;
> International agreements will be honored only so long as the cost of their violation exceeds the benefit.

It is, of course, much easier to say that we must pursue only our true national interests than to specify just what those interests are at any given time or in any specific situation. Philosophers and political thinkers of the seventeenth century were beguiled by the belief that it would some day be possible to invent an ethical calculus, whereby every political question could be answered according to the disciplines of algebra or geometry. Today we realize that even with the aid of sophisticated computers, the Cartesian dream of moving from irrefutable axioms to absolutely certain conclusions about everything human will always remain just that—a fascinating but impossible dream.

The selection of goals and the methods chosen to pursue them in the international arena—as in every other area of human activity—will always contain a large element of guesswork, intuition, and room for error. This is not the same as saying that we cannot find underlying principles or guidelines on which to base our decisions—which is why I believe adherence to the three principles enumerated above to be so critically important. They are, furthermore, closely interrelated.

If, for example, we do not believe that man will readily resort to violence, then our vast expenditures for armaments may be not only reduced but entirely eliminated. If we believe otherwise, we will endeavor (a) to maintain the ability to defend ourselves, and (b) to so order our relationships with other nations that each has more to gain from peace than from war—and knows it. And, of course, we must anticipate that they will endeavor to do the same.

It is not necessary for our international neighbors to love us, or even to trust us. All that is needed is for them to believe that it is as much to our advantage as to theirs that conflicts and competition be held below the level of overt violence—and that we have the wit to know it. This is, of course, what we should expect of others. And there are hopeful signs that the world is finally approaching this insight. It is probable that the nuclear test-ban treaty of 1963—like the "hot-line" between the Kremlin and the White House—was the direct result of the Cuban missile crisis. As one historian has written, "Russia, the United States, and all the major nations except China appeared to have learned from two decades of hostility and suspicion that no power can shape the earth to its own exclusive image, that the planet's teeming, diverse billions must live together in mutual tolerance if they would live at all." Today there is reason for hope that China, too, has learned this profound lesson.

CHAPTER THREE

The Challenges

The question most basic to international survival in the twentieth century, in my opinion, is the need for a continuously realistic appraisal of the changing currents of political intentions, ideology, patterns, and loyalties in our modern world. Are we up to date in our view of the world and its challenges? And are our policies in step with the times and the demands of these changing challenges? If we do not ask these questions and give them reasonable answers, we will fail in the world arena no matter what else we undertake, or how righteous our cause.

To put the matter in perspective, let us think back to the polarity of the world in, let us say, 1939. Who were our friends and who were our enemies? Germany under Hitler, Italy under Mussolini, Japan under Tojo, and Russia under Stalin were our enemies. Within two years there was a shift, and the Soviet Union, under heavy Nazi attacks, became our ally and friend. Then, within a scant decade, the tides changed, and we were in the icy grasp of an ideological Cold War that pitted us against the Soviet Union and all her Communist allies. The Western World was split in two by barriers of cement and steel, in the process throwing the United States into close and cordial alliance with the three nations—Germany, Japan, and Italy—which had been her strongest adversaries in World War II.

The winds of change continue to blow, and today most of

us are aware that the Communist world is no longer the monolithic block of ideologic solidarity which seemed to face us a decade ago. China and the Soviet Union are at serious odds, and almost overnight we have become committed to a national policy of diversity in our treatment of the Communist world. We perceive not only that there are significant differences in ideology and practice among the Communist nations, but also that there has been a subtle yet marked mutation in the nature of the Communist system as it has been subjected to the erosion of time, the test of practicality, and the necessity of trying to provide efficient government.

We are reminded again that there are few things more transient in world history than the mutuality of national interests; and conversely, that there is nothing quite so imperishable as the self-interest of individual states. Even the most totalitarian of governments must provide for at least the minimum needs of its people and if ancient prejudices and dogmas make this impossible, then those prejudices and dogmas will be ignored in practice—no matter how long they may linger on in political rhetoric.

In this connection, it is critically important that we pay less attention to what people say they are doing and more to what they do in actuality. There is growing understanding that many of Nikita Khrushchev's more bellicose public utterances were made for the purpose of defending his flanks against his own hawks in the Kremlin and in Peking. He was, in effect, trying to strengthen his position for making accommodations with the west. By taking literally rhetoric meant for home consumption, western statesmen did much to contribute to his ultimate downfall—and so an opportunity was lost.

It is an accepted principle of psychology that a person's deeds, observed over a period of time, are a more reliable guide to what that person really wants in the world than any purely verbal declarations about his ambitions. This is also a sound principle in dealing with nations.

Our most important problem in the world arena is the re-defining of our own national interests in terms of the realities, and not the myths, of what will soon be the last quarter of the twentieth century. The success with which we meet this problem depends in large measure, I believe, on the accuracy with which we perceive and understand the world around us, particularly that part of the world which we still may be inclined to think of as hostile.

EASTERN EUROPE AND THE COMMUNIST EMPIRE

There is, perhaps, no better showcase of the shifting nature of the Communist world today than the handful of nations comprising Eastern Europe. Here, on a broad band of territory stretching from the Baltic to the Black Sea, bordered on the West by Germany and on the East by Russia, live 100 million people who for a quarter-century have been the forced partners of the Soviet Union in an historic experiment in radical socialism, imposed upon them by the brute force of World War II and its disruptive aftermath. The people of Eastern Europe, occupying as they do the buffer zone between East and West, are by nature culturally independent and by heritage fiercely nationalistic. It is only to be expected, therefore, that the veneer of communism should wear thin first in this historically volatile area.

I have had a good many years of personal association with this part of the world. In the years before World War II, while still a college student, I traveled through Poland, Slovakia, and Hungary, and, in fact, was at one point arrested briefly by the Nazi Gestapo in Danzig. Shortly before the war my father became American minister to Hungary, where he later was interned for a short period after delivering declarations of war on behalf of the various British Commonwealth nations and after the rupturing of our relations there. After the War, I returned to Eastern Europe myself as a Foreign Service officer and established the American Consulate General at Bratislava, Czechoslovakia. While I was there, the Communists came to power in a putsch, and I had the very useful and disagreeable experience of dealing on a day-to-day basis with the new Communist government. It was during these years, too, that my younger son was born in Vienna. Later, after leaving the Foreign Service, I returned to Eastern Europe again as vice president of the International Rescue Committee to assist refugees in Austria at the time of the Hungarian Revolution of 1956. In the years since, I have returned to Eastern Europe many times to observe the changes that are taking place.

What we see in Eastern Europe, I believe, is the whole evolutionary spectrum of communism—from its unhappy origins, through its development as an ascendant system of radical social organization and control, and now to its decline as an ideology which can only survive by adopting many of the attributes of capitalism. The Russians themselves acknowledged this when they resorted, in Czechoslovakia, to the use of brute force to stifle the evolutionary forces that were swiftly moving there.

The fascinating fact here is that, while in 1948 no actual Russian soldiers were needed in Czechoslovakia to impose communism, it took more than a half million Russian and Warsaw Pact soldiers to reimpose it in 1968 after Czechoslovakia had had twenty years of Communist rule.

We must recognize that for Eastern Europe—as indeed for most of the world—the writings of Karl Marx and Friedrich Engels have virtually no relevance to today's world. They are as out of date as Ptolemy's charts would be for an astronaut. The history of Eastern Europe is a case study of the fact that social revolution in the industrial age just does not happen according to the tidy but violent Hegelian prophecies of nineteenth century theorists.

To be sure, there was what appeared to be a classic Hegelian-Marxist clash at the outset, and it came to some parts of Eastern Europe sooner than others. I personally remember in Poland the spectacle of peasants in the fields dropping to their knees to kiss the hands of strolling aristocrats and their guests in the late 1930s. I can remember staying at a house where the butler was in the hospital as the result of being kicked downstairs by his employer following a household dispute. It became clear to me then that the pendulum of social justice some day was going to swing sharply to the left in Eastern Europe, although I had no idea how far to the left. But what happened after the initial swing was not according to the script of Marx and Engels—or even of Lenin and Stalin.

The plain historic fact is that Marxism was conceived almost exclusively as a negative ideology, designed as an Hegelian antithesis of nineteenth century capitalism. It had no real or rational internal theory of economics, other than the abolition of the concept of property as we know it and the notion that the means of production should be communally or publicly owned. But as an economic theory, it was sadly lacking in detail as to how such a communally owned society would operate, and, most important, what forces and motivations would keep it running.

Thus, in Eastern Europe as well as in the Soviet Union itself, the motivation was supplied and imposed artificially through the political system, during the era which we are coming to recognize as the second or Stalinist phase of communism. This era lasted nearly three decades in the Soviet Union and one decade in Eastern Europe—drawing to a close, more or less, about 1957, following the Hungarian, Polish, and East German uprisings.

There is no doubt that the Stalinist period yielded great results, at enormous human cost and only after painful fits and starts and many miscalculations. But the undeniable proof is there to see: the Soviet Union and its satellite states did become, to varying degrees, modern industrial nations, with independent capacities for meeting at least the primary requirements of a specialized modern economy. Whether similar results might have been achieved without the messianic and sadly maniacal onslaught of communism is one of those historical "if's" to which there can never be a true answer.

In any event, there were very definite basic reforms which emerged like the Phoenix out of the second stage of communism. We must understand these advances if we are to understand the larger question of the future course of communism as an ideology and evaluate our response to that changing course.

I have said that communism is based on an archaic and negative doctrine and that for this reason it lacks any coherent internal dynamic for perpetuating itself. It began, in its first stage, on the Hegelian theory that the future can be projected as a reaction to the past or the present, and progressed to a second stage of reform and progress imposed by political regimentation, there being no system of internal economic forces to assure achievement of its goals. Granting the evidence of Communist achievement during the second stage in Eastern Europe, we must then consider the apparent evolution of a third stage of communism, which I believe is already upon us in the satellite nations of Eastern Europe and will soon confront the Communist parties of Asia.

If we were to label this third stage, I suppose it might be meaningful and accurate to call it the converging stage in the evolution of communism. For, basically, what is happening is that the Communist nations, lacking their own internal motivating forces, are drifting further and further away from radical economics and back toward the center of the political spectrum in their quest for guiding principles which will make their societies work.

The reasons for this drift to convergence are interesting. Basically, they result from the fact that communism has always had within itself the seeds of its own destruction. Having achieved the reforms which fill basic human needs for housing, food, and health, it finds that, with its people better educated and with their basic needs satisfied, it is confronted with increasing demands for human comfort and fulfillment —for freedom to worship and talk, to travel, to work where and as one chooses, to practice one's faith, and to accumulate a little property to leave for one's children—all desires which conflict directly with the political manipulation required to keep the Communist system going. Having created the educated citizenry it needed to survive in a scientific era, communism finds itself increasingly at odds with a populace which is less and less tolerant of regimentation as a way of life and the ideological strait jackets which attempt to hold them back from grasping the world as it is. Increasingly, the Communist regimes are finding themselves at odds with the young and the enlightened.

Three years ago, the *New York Times* quoted a rather poignant statement by a university professor in Warsaw, himself obviously the product of another generation, who was surveying modern Polish youth with wonder and some misgiving: "They laugh at us and what we created for them," he said. "They know only the advantages and forget what we suffered to create them. Without us they would never have seen the university. We have opened for everybody what only the rich had before. They accept it, but they don't know what it cost us."

There was no better proof and confirmation of this alienation of the young than the Hungarian Revolution of 1956, an event which I had occasion to view at rather close quarters, actually being at the Bridge at Andau. For in that case it was the students and workers—the traditional allies of earlier Communist uprisings—who in this case fought a Communist regime almost to a standstill. And, interestingly enough, it was the shopkeepers and former middle classes—the traditional enemies of communism—who on that occasion sat on their hands.

Thus we see that there are many internal forces at work today in the third stage of Communist development for which Karl Marx and Friedrich Engels made no provision: alienation, impatience, economic and spiritual discontent, and, simply, the natural desires and aspirations of man.

The Communist regimes learned in the '50s through the hard lessons of Poznan, Warsaw, and Budapest, that these internal pressures cannot simply be met by continued or increased political regimentation. And so they have, slowly and gradually, begun, in effect, to rebuild the Communist world to take account of human nature.

Slowly, and inexorably, the Communist states are being forced to move away from the artificial controls of political regimentation and substitute the normal interplay of human instincts and desires as the most sure criteria for public policy. In the basic area of economics, where these changes in viewpoint manifest themselves earliest, this means that there is to an increasing degree substitution of market demands and consumer choices for production quotas, of interest payments as an incentive to investment, and of merit pay and bonuses to reward talent and initiative.

We might think, at first glance, that the result would be something that looks like a capitalistic society. This, of course, is not the case, but it is clear that the evolving system is a substantial mutation of the original Marxist economy. One very apt label being applied to it is the term "Market Socialism." I have noted with interest that economists from both sides of the Iron Curtain have met to discuss the theory of convergence of the two basic economic systems: the Western market economy and the Eastern centrally planned economy. It is this concept which inspires my own label of converging for the third stage of Communist evolution.

THE FUTURE OF COMMUNISM

I want to emphasize I am not suggesting that the point of convergence is now at hand, or that the Communist states have been totally reformed. In many respects, in fact, the rigid authoritarian political system remains as strong as ever, as the people of Prague have more than once been reminded. But I am speaking here in terms of long-range trends and evolutionary processes. In that context there are some very interesting signs indeed of movement, from revolution to devolution to a form of evolution.

Consider, for example, the question of consumer credit, which has only recently made its appearance as a part of the supply and demand system in the Soviet Union and Eastern Europe. This is a very significant development, for it opens to the average citizen the possibility of purchasing goods he previously could not have dreamed of owning, and this in turn commits the State economy to producing more and more of the sort of consumer goods he wants to buy.

Installment buying was first introduced in the Soviet Union in 1959 and has spread since into all of Eastern Europe. Under the Soviet system, the buyer is generally required to limit himself to credit equaling not more than four months average wages. The payments are collected directly from his employer who acts as the guarantor of the debt. The down payment must cover not less than 25 percent of the total price and service charges are quite low, not exceeding 2 percent for a debt extending over twelve months.

In Rumania, which from a domestic viewpoint is perhaps the least liberal of the satellites, down payments range up to 40 percent and repayment is required in six months. In Poland, where even automobiles can be purchased on credit, the terms are more liberal and average consumer debts are extended nineteen months.

One notable result of these policies has been stimulation of the manufacture of consumer goods in each of the satellite nations. Television sets, refrigerators, washing machines, and radios are being produced in increasing volume with East Germany, Czechoslovakia, and Poland leading in volume of production.

Tourism, with or without credit, is another big factor in both the economic and ideologic reorientation of the Eastern European states. The contacts made and information exchanged and new interests aroused by such travel will contribute immensely, I believe, to the gradual erosion of barriers between East and West.

On the heels of tourism comes trade, and there is much evidence that the countries of Eastern Europe want to increase their trade with the West. One symbol of American commercial penetration to date which particularly struck me on a recent visit was the availability of Coca-Cola in Bulgaria. However, Coca-Cola is really only a symbol of what might be, because our trade with the satellite nations is lamentably low. A major impediment in each case is the absence of nondiscriminatory or so-called most-favored nation tariff or trading treatment, by which we would assure each of the Communist and satellite nations that it could trade with us on the same terms we extend to the rest of the world.

An interesting case in point is that of Rumania which, more than any other satellite nation, is displaying an independent foreign policy which borders almost on open defiance of the Soviet Union. Her trade with the Soviet Union has steadily decreased, and she seeks new trading partners in the West; already 30 percent of her trade is with Western Europe. But Rumania's trade with the United States is infinitesimal. As in the other satellite countries, the lack of most-favored nation privileges is a serious—if not fatal—barrier. There are other special problems in the case of Rumania, for

Rumanian officials consider that they burned their fingers badly in their negotiations with the Firestone Company several years ago for the construction of two synthetic rubber plants. Firestone later withdrew from the negotiations because of pressure from a competitor, pressure which was exerted through a campaign in the United States which appealed to emotional anticommunism. As a result, Rumania will be chary of such negotiations in the future.

"LIBERAL" COMMUNISM

Turning away from the field of economics, I should like to add to this survey of the new era in the evolution of communism by taking note of certain other changes in orientation which strike me as particularly significant.

One general observation is that political oppression has significantly declined. Even in Hungary, where the abortive revolt of 1956 and Russian repression is still a very real memory, the reign of terror is over. The police no longer knock on the door at midnight to arrest and torture citizens who run afoul of the regime. And political opponents no longer fear execution. Repression is still a fact of life, but it is less obvious, less direct, and less brutal. As communism in Eastern Europe mellows and enters the era of convergence, the most obvious techniques of regimentation are falling into disuse.

Another very significant fact, I believe, is that the Catholic Church is retaining its strength in Eastern Europe and in some cases even improving its position.

It is an interesting and frequently overlooked fact that in many of the Communist countries of Eastern Europe, the churches and the clergy are directly supported and subsidized by the state. This results from the fact that the Communist regimes first of all deprived the churches of the lands and properties which for so long had been their source of support and financial independence. Subsequently, the Communist governments in several instances launched on a clear policy of caesaro-papism, which simply means using the church for the purposes of the state. The process has also been described as a kind of one-sided separation of church and state, in which the churches have no right to interfere with the political life of the country, but there is no prohibition against government intervention in the affairs of the church.

My impression is that this process has been carried to greater extremes, as we might expect, in those countries which historically had a greater commitment to national Orthodox churches than to Roman Catholicism with its allegiance to the Pope. In the Socialist Republic of Rumania, for example, the salaries and subsidies paid by the government may be suspended if there is evidence of "undemocratic attitudes" on the part of the clergy. Also, the government may simply annul the appointment of clergymen and teachers at religious institutions "in the interest of public order or state security." It is worth noting, too, that the salaries paid the clergy in Rumania are noncompetitive, with salaries for parish clergy reported in the range of twenty-eight dollars a month, which is less than the pay of a construction worker. A bishop might make as much as seventy dollars a month.

In Bulgaria, the national Orthodox church received government subsidy until the early 1950s, when the payments were suspended and the government apparently launched on a course designed to virtually eliminate the practice of religion. The Holy Synod of the Bulgarian Orthodox Church subsequently reported that its support was based almost wholly on the sale of candles. In 1963 the government added an administrative blow by decreeing that Sunday was to be a regular workday and that different days of the week were to be designated as days of rest in the different administrative· districts of the country. Bulgaria is thus the extreme example of state domination of religious activity in Eastern Europe. But the church is still there—a prime example of Marxist-

Leninist dogma yielding to pragmatic realities.

In the Roman Catholic countries of Eastern Europe, the evidence seems to be that the practice of state subsidy has been resorted to as a necessity because the church fulfilled such an important role, but that the imposition of caesaropapism has been much less complete and much less effective. In Poland, for example, the clergy receive stipends paid from the income obtained from confiscated church property. They also are paid fees for the performance of religious services in state facilities, such as hospitals, prisons, and sanatoriums. But when the state attempts to collect its tribute in return, in the form of bureaucratic interference in the training of the clergy, it encounters continuing firm and outspoken opposition.

In Czechoslovakia, the state has succeeded to a greater extent than in most other countries. It has made the church depend almost wholly on the government for economic support and in return the state controls the number of persons permitted to study for the priesthood and exercises veto power over clerical appointments. But there has been a relaxation of state regimentation in recent years to the extent that some of the Czech bishops were permitted to attend the Vatican Council. A Czechoslovakian Cardinal, Dr. Josef Beran, and several other bishops and clergymen have been freed from long political imprisonment, and the government has concluded a protocol with the Vatican in which it formally acknowledges the role of the church.

In Hungary, which is the most eastern country in Europe with a Catholic majority, the church suffered renewed oppression following the abortive revolution of 1956, in which the clergy were accused of playing an important role. Now, however, the position of the church has improved since the signing of a protocol with the Vatican in 1964. There is no overt oppression although there is no question but the church still must be responsive to state control. But, on balance, it seems to me the church has not lost any ground and in some cases it has clearly gained.

These then are the high points of Eastern Europe today: a Communist satellite zone in a condition of flux and change, as it enters a distinctly new phase of ideological evolution. Old techniques of repression have had to be abandoned, new recognition has been given to normal human aspirations and desires, new opportunities for trade and tourism present themselves, and an older generation of doctrinaire Communists is yielding to a new wave of youth and experimentation.

How should we in the West react to these changes and what are their implications for the long-range evolution of East-West relations? It seems plain to me that we have a great opportunity and that if we conduct ourselves with wisdom, imagination, and restraint—and avoid the ideological rigidities of the 1950s and '60s—we can go a long way toward resolving the great ideological cold war of the twentieth century.

We have heard of the revolution of rising expectations in the developing countries of the world. The Communist countries of Eastern Europe are caught, it seems to me, in a counterrevolution of rising expectations.

All men have certain natural drives which, as we have seen in the political and economic spheres, include the desire for freedom, for human contact, and for property. As standards of living improve in Eastern Europe, as adequate housing, health care, and education become generally available, as communication and direct exposure to Western societies increases through tourists who visit from the West, these drives will become stronger. They will force Communist governments to change to adjust to these drives. The first demand may be freedom to choose one's work. The inevitable result will be freedom to choose how to dispose of the gains of work —more choice, in other words, in what to buy and where to travel. And eventually, although this end is certainly not yet in sight, there will undoubtedly be a demand for freedom of choice in politics.

I am convinced, therefore, that time is on our side in Eastern Europe. The trend there is toward freedom—and not away from it. Communism is changing to accommodate this trend, changing more slowly in some countries—more rapidly in others. It seems obvious to me that we can best hasten this erosion within the Communist world by increasing contact at every level, and in every sphere of activity, between the countries of the West and those of Eastern Europe. We have an opportunity to avoid the mistakes of the postwar era to which I have already referred—and once more pursue our true national interests.

There are some definite political steps which we should be prepared to take in response to the situation. We should, for example, enact legislation to promote East-West trade, granting to the nations of Eastern Europe the equal or nondiscriminatory ("most-favored nation") tariff treatment they so much desire. What this will mean in actual trade possibilities until the United States has solved its basic balance of payments problem is problematical. But at least we can demonstrate that whatever the restrictive trade policies in which we engage, the motives are purely economic and not political or ideological.

There will be other clear opportunities for political and diplomatic action on our part as time goes on, particularly if we are fortunate enough to be able to take steps in such areas as arms control. But the essential, continuing challenge is a philosophical one and it is one we will have learned to anticipate and respond to effectively if we fully appreciate what is now transpiring in Eastern Europe—and perhaps Asia. Basically, it is a challenge to be sensitive and responsive to change and evolution, and to free ourselves of stereotyped misconceptions and out-of-date notions. We must learn to contemplate the realities, rather than the mythologies, of world affairs in this last portion of the twentieth century.

We must all learn this lesson—Americans, Russians, Chinese, and every other great power—if only because that is the only way to assure that there will be a twenty-*first* century.

One of the realities we must face is that the world is not static. It never has been and, as we have already commented, the pace of change in the twentieth century is far greater than ever before in human history. Furthermore, the tempo is still increasing. The only thing about tomorrow of which we can be certain is that tomorrow will be different. It is a natural human tendency to view the world as a settled place in which what we remember from yesterday describes the reality of today.

Were he to be miraculously resurrected, a victim of the second World War, one who died perhaps fighting the hated "Japs" in the South Pacific, would be utterly unable to comprehend our present friendly relations with our former mortal enemies. Observing the Japanese cameras in the hands of his fellow Americans, seeing the Datsun and Toyota automobiles on our highways, learning that more than 80 percent of our motorcycles are of Japanese origin, he might conclude that America had lost the war. His Japanese counterpart, the former warrior for Japan's ambitious Co-prosperity Sphere, the banner under which the war was launched, might well ask why such a bloody tragedy was ever begun. Using the techniques of peaceful competition, the Japanese have become in twenty-five short years the world's third largest industrial nation—a position of eminence hardly envisioned by the most grandiose of the warlords who launched her expansionist adventures in the 1930s. What did we die for?

Times change, and people and nations change with them. Often we can influence the direction of that change; certainly that is one of the central purposes of foreign policy. But to exercise it effectively we must be clear in our minds that the Russia or China—or Germany or Japan—that we deal with today is not the one we dealt with yesterday, and certainly is not the one we will be dealing with tomorrow. Nor, indeed, are we the same. In coping with our current problems, we must remind ourselves that time is also a dimension and that it can be made to work for us.

The Communists have always shown a better insight in this regard than their western adversaries. During the early days of the revolution in Russia, Lenin permitted virtually unopposed incursions into Red territory by White Russians and their foreign supporters. The military battle could wait, in Lenin's mind, until he had consolidated his power and firmly seized the reins of government. His strategy was described in a classic remark of the day: "The Old Man is trading space for time."

It is an axiom of Communist dogma that capitalism is in a state of perpetual disintegration, that it contains within itself the seeds of its own destruction. As previously stated, I am of the opinion that the shoe is on just the other foot. Capitalism as we know it, modern capitalism, happens to work. Communism does not. The changes and modifications in the Communist system during the next decades, accordingly, will be far more sweeping than in our own system. Whatever may be left of monolithic communism, including the Russian hegemony in Eastern Europe, will dissolve with the liberalization of economic and trade policies—a liberalization bound to occur because trying to operate a tightly-controlled, centralized economy in the modern era of computers and world-wide markets is like commanding water to run uphill.

Paradoxically, the Communists' dogmatic confidence in the inevitable destruction-from-within of their adversaries has made them relatively cautious in their foreign policy. If victory is certain, it may be all right to help history along, but why risk everything on one throw of the dice when you expect to win anyhow? What made the Cuban missile crisis so threatening was that it represented an abrupt departure from this normal Russian caution. Today, the USSR has the capability of inflicting far more destruction on the United States with intercontinental missiles than she could have done with intermediate range missiles in the early 1960s. Russia took an enormous risk to establish a parity of destruction by putting IRBMs in Cuba when her developing ICBM capacity was certain to accomplish the same objective within a very few years.

It was this sudden apparent departure from the normal Russian chess game which disturbed sophisticated observers, more even than the missiles themselves. There is reason to believe that the danger inherent in that impulsive departure from the normal Russian game plan had much to do with Premier Khrushchev's fall from power; and that in fact, as previously suggested, it resulted more from internal political struggles within the Kremlin than from aggressive intentions toward the United States. With this exception, however, Russian policy has been remarkably consistent. The Russians have rarely failed to pursue an opportunity; they maintain a continuous pressure in all the areas where they conceive their national interests to lie. But they are patient. If the time is not propitious, if the resistance is strong, if the risk is too high—well, tomorrow is another day; they believe they can afford to wait and try again.

This patience has certainly enabled them to accomplish many of their foreign policy objectives. It has also served the cause of world peace—which, in our era, means world survival. The USSR has, for example, now achieved naval parity in the Mediterranean. I do not view this with as much alarm as some other observers. Given the size of Russia's population, her natural resources, and her geographic position, such a condition should not be too surprising. Had our positions been reversed, had there been a Russian Sixth Fleet in the Caribbean over the years, we would certainly have demanded a similar parity and increased our own naval forces in the area as soon as we had the power to do so. What is important is that such pursuits of national policy be accomplished peacefully and that their overall effect is to make outright war less, rather than more, likely.

Free passage through the Dardanelles Straits into the Mediterranean has been an objective of Russian policy throughout modern history. The Russians have reacted to foreign efforts to restrict their right of passage much as we would react to an attempt by Canada to control our own access to the St. Lawrence Seaway. This concern of the Russians, in fact, had much to do with the genesis of the first World War. The German-Austro-Hungarian *Drang nach Osten* through the Balkans and Turkey threatened Russia's traditional desire for security in the Bosporus and the Dardanelles and led indirectly to the anti-Austrian activities in Serbia, which ultimately brought about the assassination of Archbuke Francis Ferdinand at Sarajevo, and the Great War.

Today, Russia has free passage through the Dardanelles, her fleet is in the Mediterranean, yet Turkey remains a sovereign power—and there has been no war. I consider this an improvement over the events of 1914–1918.

Patience in the pursuit of foreign policy objectives, in short, can permit many of those objectives to be accomplished without resort to overt force. It is the use of time as a dimension of policy. The Communists—Chinese no less than Russian—have shown themselves adept at exploiting this fourth dimension of time. Is there any reason why this technique should be left only to the Communists? Russia is changing, China is changing, Eastern Europe and Asia are equally in flux. We must learn to base our policies—the methods by which we seek to achieve our international objectives—not merely on what we find confronting us in the international arena today, but on what we can reasonably expect to face a decade or more hence.

Not only do we often fail to anticipate change, we often fail to recognize even the changes which have already occurred. Thanks to the ubiquitousness of American motion pictures, there are millions of people in the world who still think of America in terms of gangsters and the Wild West; in fact, I have a friend from Chicago who recently told me of being driven through Beirut by a chauffeur who solemnly inquired whether, by any chance, he knew Al Capone. Such misconceptions may be quaint and amusing, but they can lead to catastrophic miscalculations if permitted to persist as hidden or unconscious assumptions about other nations in the formulation of national policy.

The importance of considering time as a crucial dimension in the formulation of policy is difficult to make clear—and impossible to overemphasize. Perhaps we can make an analogy with the motion picture mentioned above. There is in actuality no such thing as a "moving picture." A strip of motion picture film held in the hand reveals nothing but a series of still pictures identical with those you might take with your own camera. It is only when the strip of film is run through a projector at a very specific speed that the images begin to move and we see a replica of the action which took place in front of the motion picture camera. In other words, the dimension of time has been added, and that new dimension transforms a collection of static images into a vital representation of the world we live in—a world of change and motion.

In the conduct of foreign policy, we frequently have too many frozen images and too few mental projectors with which to set them in motion.

We must learn to live with time, to work with time and to make time work for us. Impatience has always been an American characteristic, but it is one that should be curbed. If we can't change one still picture into another without war and violent action, it is better to forego the change of pictures and settle for a lot of little changes in the direction we want. And when it comes to communism, time is running on our side because of communism's own weaknesses and lack of long term appeal to people under it.

CHAPTER FOUR

How Our Foreign Policy
Is Made

The makers of foreign policy, like the directors of any enterprise, are continuously confronted with the problem of dealing simultaneously with short-term emergencies and long-term objectives. The Situation Room of the White House, with its hot line to the Kremlin, might be compared to the emergency ward of a hospital. Someone is on duty day and night to deal with the hundred and one afflictions which befall people living in a crowded and often violent world. The emergency ward is not, however, the place to deal with such long-term problems as how to finance the hospital over the next ten years, what kind of standards to set for admission to the medical board, and so forth. There must be a division of labor. Otherwise, the confusion between long-term and short-term challenges will lead to diastrous handling of both the emergency patient and the future of the hospital.

This is nowhere illustrated more clearly—nor tragically—than in the development of our intervention in Vietnam. In its initial reaction to the so-called Pentagon Papers in mid–1971 *Time* magazine observed:

As the documents bared the planning process, they also demolished any lingering faith that the nation's weightiest decisions are made by deliberative men calmly examining all the implications of a policy and then carefully laying out this reasoning in depth. The proliferation of papers, the cabled requests for clarification, the briskness of language but not of logic, convey an impression of harassed men, thinking and writing too quickly and sometimes being mystified at the enemy's refusal to conform to official projections.

There is a humorous remark often heard in Washington that the word, "clarification," is bureaucratic jargon for "filling up the background with so many facts that the foreground sinks out of sight." The results, as in the tragedy of Vietnam, are usually far from amusing. As the *Time* editors also noted:

Each step seems to have been taken almost in desperation because the preceding step had failed to check the crumbling of the South Vietnamese government and its troops—and despite frequently expressed doubts that the next move would be much more effective. Yet the bureaucracy, the Pentagon Papers indicate, always demanded new options; each option was to apply more force. Each tightening of the screw created a position that must be defended; once committed, the military pressure must be maintained. A pause, it was agreed, would reveal lack of resolve, embolden the Communists and further demoralize the South Vietnamese. Almost no one said: "Wait—where are we going? Should we turn back?"

There were, in fact, a few such voices in the executive branch—notably George Ball in the State Department and John McCone at the Central Intelligence Agency—but their views were almost wholly submerged by "the system." The question, Where are we going? was most frequently raised in the Senate. I was amongst those early and few ones who strongly opposed the bombing of North Vietnam, principally because I believed that it would be counterproductive; i.e., instead of weakening Hanoi's will to continue the conflict, the net effect of the bombing would be to strengthen their determination.

Study of the reports on U.S. strategic bombing of Germany during the Second World War had made me deeply skeptical about the effectiveness of bombing in reducing a country's capability for industrial production—even in an advanced industrial nation like Germany, let alone a relatively primitive nation such as Vietnam. Those same studies had also convinced me that such bombing actually tends to improve the people's morale, in the military sense of that word; in other words, bombing increases a people's hatred of their enemy and heightens national solidarity and determination to resist at all costs. This was familiar to all of us as we watched the heroic reaction of the British people to the German blitz during the Battle of Britain and I could see no reason to assume that the people of North Vietnam were made of less sterner stuff simply because their skin happens to be yellow.

Congressional critics of the Vietnam involvement, like their counterparts in the press, were usually informed that, due to the requirements of national security, we could not be given all the facts; but that if we had access to all the information on which the government was basing its decisions, we would no doubt find our misgivings assuaged. It was somewhat ironic, therefore, to discover that during the whole period the head of the CIA was insisting that American intelligence indicated that the bombings were indeed counterproductive (as the CIA had also accurately forecast), and that intelligence estimates strongly suggested that "with the exception of Cambodia, it is likely that no nation would quickly succumb to communism." Our own intelligence agency, in short, agreed with many members of the Senate Foreign Relations Committee, other members of the Congress, and concerned citizens in private life about the lack of wisdom of both the bombing tactics and the domino theory which held that Vietnam was the plug which, if pulled by Hanoi, would open all of Southeast Asia to communism. Yet none of this seemed able to affect those in charge of U.S. policy making concerning Vietnam.

Many books have been and will be written about the U.S. adventure in Vietnam. We will be many years sorting out the short and long-term consequences of Vietnam not only upon our foreign policy but upon almost every other facet of American life. It is not my purpose to attempt that analysis in these brief pages. Nor is it my purpose to attempt to apportion praise or blame among particular decision makers. The search for heroes and villains in the evolution of public policy—as echoed, for example, in the catch phrase of the early 1950s, "Who lost China?"—serves primarily to distract our attention from the mechanism of decision making and from the errors in basic philosophy which permitted the mistakes to happen, or, in the light of historical hindsight, seem to make many of them virtually inevitable.

The difference, too, with regard to the treatment of the China hands in the 1950s and the Vietnam policy hands in the 1970s is shown by the positions held today by some of them —such, for example, as the presidency of the world's largest financial institution, the presidency of our largest foundation, and the editorship of the leading foreign policy journal, *Foreign Affairs*. The reason here may be that the so-called Eastern Establishment had little to do with China but a lot to do with developing our Vietnam policy. And the Eastern Establishment apparently looks after its own. I say this, too, as one generally identified as a member of that Establishment!

As former General Matthew B. Ridgway (who was an early opponent of our Vietnam involvement) has written, "It serves no useful purpose to label all [past] decisions as mistakes, however loud the voices of those who do so. Right or wrong, the decisions were made in good faith in accordance with our constitutional procedures by civilian authority."

It may be argued that in the case of Vietnam the government's adherence to "constitutional procedures," while conforming to the letter of the Constitution frequently violated its spirit—with regard to the war-making powers of the Congress, for instance, or in the use made of the Gulf of Tonkin resolution in claiming Congressional support for subsequent escalation of the conflict. Similar legalisms have been employed by governments in the past. The Korean conflict, for example, is still not recognized by official documents as a war involving the United States; it was merely a "police action" undertaken by the United Nations.

More important by far than the motivations of individual political leaders or foreign policy specialists, and of the methods they choose to employ, is the question: how can the mechanism of decision making be changed to avoid such catastrophies in the future?

Equally important—or perhaps really part of the same need for reforming the decision making process—is the question: how can we prevent the decision makers from losing sight of the woods for the trees? I have already stressed the importance of a nation's foreign policy having clear-cut goals, within its capacity to attain, and related to its true national interests. To cite General Ridgway once more:

> In the field of foreign relations, each and every one of our major political objectives should be seen to lie clearly within the zone of our vital national interests.
>
> In each case the military objectives should be in conformity with and subordinate to the political objective.
>
> Vietnam was, in my opinion, a case which violated both these prescriptions. The stated political objectives were numerous, tenuous and by no means clearly within the zone of our vital interests, while the military objectives were not subordinate to the political but at one state, at least, rather tended to dictate the political objectives.

These observations by a former commanding general in Europe and Korea suggest—at least to me—that there is no basic disagreement between serious students of foreign policy, military or civilian, in the executive branch or in the Congress, about where wisdom lies in these matters. The real question is how, given these insights, we could have continued to act so unwisely.

Whatever the final outcome in Vietnam, and without regard to whether the expenditure was worth the cost, I believe it can be said that at least one point has been made: no country can ever again assume that America will not fight. Proponents of American intervention in Vietnam have frequently argued that Vietnam, like Korea, was a result of miscalculation on the part of our enemies. We surprised them by our resistance in Korea, according to this analysis, and so they attempted a different approach in Vietnam. Instead of an invasion, there would be a "war of national liberation," which the Americans—and the rest of the non-Communist world—would be ill-equipped by tradition to fight. It is now quite obvious to foreign analysts that American policy is, to say the least, highly unpredictable. No Communist power can ignore the costs of Vietnam—proportionately far higher for the North Vietnamese than for us—nor can it be entirely certain that our future response will be any less violent. To whatever extent Vietnam was a test of will between the Communist and non-Communist world, it has to be viewed as a standoff. It is doubtful that either side will soon demand a rematch.

What, then, are the reasonable objectives of U.S. foreign policy after Vietnam? They are, I submit, what they have always been: (1) to achieve a workable peace among nations; (2) to improve the quality of life throughout the world so as to reduce the pressures which threaten that peace; and (3) to maintain our own strength in sufficient measure to defend ourselves, if necessary, until the first two objectives have been achieved.

Reaching these objectives, however, will depend as much on the mechanisms we employ in our efforts to achieve them as on the objectives themselves. We have seen too many examples of how the means have a way of becoming the ends in pursuit of foreign policy objectives—most recently and perhaps most poignantly in the case of Vietnam. It is essential, therefore, to understand how our foreign policy—whatever it may be—is actually formulated and conducted.

THE MECHANISMS OF FOREIGN POLICY

Probably the only extended period in our history when there was no debate going on between Congress and the executive branch over the proper course of U.S. foreign policy occurred in the years immediately after the start of the Revolution —and then only because there was no separate executive branch. From 1775 to 1789, Congress exercised sole control of foreign policy. The Committee of Foreign Affairs (1777–1781) and the Department of Foreign Affairs (1781—1789), the precursors of our modern State Department, were agents of the Congress and reported directly to it, much like the General Accounting Office of today.

When the executive and judicial branches of the government were created at the Constitutional Convention of 1789, the direction of foreign policy was placed primarily in the hands of the president and he was provided by the first Congress with a cabinet department to assist him. Presidents, members of Congress, secretaries of state, and historians have been debating ever since just how much power over foreign policy it was intended for the Congress to retain.

The Constitution gave the president power to make appointments, receive foreign ambassadors, and conclude treaties with other nations. But very important powers were retained by the Congress to act as a check on possible abuses of presidential power in these matters. The president's appointments to office, including ambassadorships, had to be confirmed by the Senate, which also had to ratify treaties before they could take effect. Congress, of course, also controlled authorizations and appropriations, which meant that it could "veto" individual projects by refusing the funds to carry them out.

This potential veto power has been exercised but rarely, and there is an amusing example from history which demonstrates its limitations. Amusing today, that is; I doubt that many congressmen found it amusing at the time.

When President Theodore Roosevelt proposed to "show the flag" by sending a flotilla of U.S. naval vessels—"the Great White Fleet"—on a trip around the world, there was considerable opposition to the project in Congress. Many members considered it provocatory, a resurgence of the manifest destiny philosophy of an earlier decade.

While Congress debated, opponents of the president's plan felt confident that nothing would be done without their consent because there was simply not enough money in the Navy's budget to finance such a tour de force. It would require a special appropriation.

What they overlooked, however, was the fact that while President Roosevelt did not have enough money to send the fleet around the world, he had enough to send it *half*-way around the world—which, in his characteristically decisive fashion, he promptly did. This left the Congress with the alternative of leaving it there or appropriating money to bring the fleet home. A rather limited choice.

In modern times, the Congress of the United States has been confronted with an ever-increasing number of these Hobson's choices, and while the Teddy Roosevelt example may be from this vantage point in history merely amusing, others have been tragic. The example still before us is the war in Vietnam. "War," of course, is an imprecise term. Since the Constitution reserves the power to declare war exclusively to the Congress, and since Congress has neither made such a declaration nor been asked by the president to do so, it follows by the peculiar logic of our times that the hostilities in which we have suffered tens of thousands of casualties is not a "war." Similarly, the Korean hostilities, as previously noted, are still officially a "police action," not a "war."

What this recent history tells us is that words, even words written into our constitution, can always be circumvented—and will be circumvented whenever the realities of power permit. Moreover, any modern president is in a position to so influence events as to confront the people, through their representatives in the Congress, with an accomplished fact about which very little can be done. It required no act of Congress, for example, to permit President Eisenhower to send a contingent of marines to Lebanon, nor for President Johnson to send U.S. military forces to the Dominican Republic.

As I have already indicated, I believe in strong leadership enlightened by firm and clear goals—as clear, at least, as goals and objectives can be in the complex interrelationships among nations. As Aristotle long ago observed, "Our discussion will be adequate if it has as much clearness as the subject matter admits of. . . . [we should] look for precision in each class of things just so far as the nature of the subject admits." No doubt as much harm has been done by dogmatism through the years as by vagueness or indecisiveness.

I do believe, however, that in the United States in this specific period of time, the pendulum has swung farther toward executive power—without real accountability to the people's legislative representatives—than any nation can afford if it intends to remain a democratic republic.

This is not the result of any sinister motives on the part of presidents, or anyone else in the executive branch. The situation has arisen as the aftermath of two world wars, the increasing complexity of international affairs, and especially the technological revolution, which has frighteningly shortened the time available for decision making.

The fact most frequently cited to demonstrate the latter point is that if the USSR were to launch a full-scale nuclear-missile assault on the United States, our leaders would have somewhere between fifteen to thirty minutes to decide on our military response; by the end of that time, Washington and New York, along with other major cities and perhaps one hundred million of our people would no longer exist. No one quarrels with the need to give the president, the Pentagon, and all of the executive branch broad and decisive powers to deal with such an emergency. What concerns us here is not the final apocalypse but the myraid events which will either lead to it, or head it off. Our government's handling of the Cuban missile crisis, for example, was in large part admirable. But it was in vivid contrast to the series of small mistakes and willful oversights which led up to the Bay of Pigs.

Not only has the pendulum of decision making swung from the legislative toward the executive branch, but American foreign policy has also been increasingly formulated and directed by the president through personal aides and representatives who are apart from the formal processes envisioned by the Constitution. Presidents from Wilson to Nixon have generally depended more on executive assistants in the White House—men such as Colonel House, McGeorge Bundy, Walt Rostow, and Henry Kissinger—than on their own appointed secretaries of state, let alone the career Foreign Service. This tendency has been by no means confined to the United States. It arises from the desire of most modern heads of state to conduct foreign policy directly and personally. As someone has remarked, the era of Talleyrands and Metternichs is over.

There is no question concerning the president's constitutional right to do so, but it has the effect of further narrowing the base of decision making and, in my opinion, greatly increases the probability of uncorrected error becoming a permanent and unseen part of our on-going foreign policy.

Furthermore, as the chairman of the Foreign Relations Committee, Senator Fulbright, has frequently pointed out, secretaries of state are at least to some extent answerable to the Congress in a way which White House aides are not.

THE GROWTH OF BUREAUCRACY

Under President Washington, the Department of State consisted of the secretary, a chief clerk, three ordinary clerks, and a translator—for a total of six persons. Even in 1870 the personnel of the State Department numbered only 53. In 1909, the number of government employees concerned primarily with foreign policy had grown only to 202. But with the advent of World War I, the personnel roles began to expand by almost geometric progression. At the end of World War II, the total stood at nearly 6,000. While the population of the country increased some fortyfold between 1789 and 1948, the number of State Department employees concerned with foreign policy increased nearly a thousandfold.

It is an accepted principle of philosophy that a point can be reached when a difference in degree becomes so great that it imperceptibly turns into a difference in kind. Although their formal function under the constitution remains the same, there is an obvious difference between six men responsible to the president for the conduct of foreign policy, and many hundreds or thousands of men and women engaged in the day-to-day conduct of foreign affairs, most of whom will never be personally known even to the secretary of state, let alone the president.

In theory, the formulation and direction of American foreign policy are responsibilities of the State Department, reporting to the president through the secretary of state. The carrying-out of these policies is a shared responsibility between two groups which the public generally thinks of as identical, but which are in fact significantly different: the

Foreign Service and the State Department itself.

The Foreign Service consists of a corps of career officers whose primary duty is representing the United States in foreign countries and conveying back to Washington information and informed judgements about the course of events in the countries where they are stationed. Traditionally, the State Department and the Foreign Service have been manned by distinct and noninterchangeable bureaucracies. Foreign Service personnel are subject to their own system of examinations and rules of promotion, while permanent members of the State Department staff belong to the Career Civil Service and are regulated by the Civil Service Commission. This dualism has inevitably promoted much friction and jealousy. One of the major proposals of the Hoover Commission, in 1949, was for an amalgamation of the two groups. The commission recommended a single foreign affairs service which would include all State Department personnel below the rank of assistant secretary (normally a political appointee) and all Foreign Service personnel below the rank of minister. Although these steps were never entirely carried out, since the Hoover Commission the Foreign Service has been much more thoroughly under the control of the secretary of state, in contrast to the semiautonomous position it occupied during much of our history.

The continuing growth of the State Department has led to periodic reorganizations, all designed ultimately to give the secretary of state greater power to co-ordinate the labyrinth of policy information which comes to him from abroad and to relieve him of the administrative details which make it impossible to see the forest because of the trees.

Whether these numerous reorganizations have made the department a more flexible instrument of foreign policy remains a question still to be answered. Judging from their public and private remarks on the subject, most of our recent presidents have been dissatisfied. President Kennedy even took the extraordinary step of offering senior officials in the department a substantial bonus on their retirement pensions if they would agree to retire prior to the mandatory retirement age—hardly a vote of confidence by the president for his senior officials.

In any event, the State Department and the career Foreign Service are no longer the only or even the primary architects or implementers of U.S. foreign policy. The simple situation during the early years of our country when the president and the State Department alone formulated policy and attempted to carry it out disappeared long ago. The Hoover Commission Task Force on Foreign Affairs indentified no less than forty-six departments, agencies, commissions, boards, and interdepartmental councils, whose work according to the task force's report "involves some aspects of the conduct of foreign affairs." Integrating the work of these agencies into a unified instrument of policy remains one of the more serious unsolved problems of our government.

Among the more important agencies working in tandem with the State Department—and often in competition—are the National Security Council and the Central Intelligence Agency, both created by the National Security Act of 1947 as a result of our wartime experiences. This was the same year in which, for similar reasons, we began the process of bringing the traditional military services under a single umbrella by creating a Department of Defense. The National Security Council has advisory powers only, its client being the president. Its original purpose, however, was to tie together foreign policy on the one hand and the military and material means to support that policy on the other, just as the Central Intelligence Agency was assigned the role of co-ordinating the intelligence activities of the several government departments and agencies in the interest of national security.

While this is still true in theory, in actual practice the National Security Council staff frequently appears as a competitive body to the State Department in the formulation if not the actual implementation of foreign policy. It is the National Security Council staff which supports such presidential advisors as Bundy, Rostow, and Kissinger and makes them, inevitably, bureaucratic rivals of the secretary of state. No matter whether the individual holder of the office seeks to avoid such rivalry, it is inherent in the job.

The interrelationship of defense policy and foreign policy is exceedingly complex. In theory, the sole function of the defense establishment is to provide the military means to carry out the foreign policy of the United States as formulated by the president and the Congress. In actuality, the defense establishment cannot help but have a profound effect on the determination of policy. The adequacy of the means available to us inevitably has an effect on the ends we choose to pursue. The U.S. troop build-up in Vietnam beginning in 1965, for example, was perhaps the most impressive logistical exercise in military history. More than 100,000 troops—with full equipment—were moved 10,000 miles in 100 days, arriving ready for combat. Had the Vietnamese conflict reached the level of 1965 ten years earlier, or even five years, the U.S. response would have been different if for no other reason than the fact that we simply did not have the military capability. In saying this, I am not adopting the simplistic view that since armaments are necessary for war, the best road to peace is unilateral disarmament. My only point is that the existence of military capability widens the range of choice available to policy makers, and therefore has a direct effect on foreign policy decisions. And a limited capability can be as dangerous as a large one; if, for example, our defense forces were to be reduced to missile silos and nuclear submarines—if these were our only means of responding to aggression—the risk of nuclear war would be greatly increased.

Since the various defense reorganization acts of the 1940s and 1950s, responsibility for carrying out military policy has rested with the secretary of defense acting under the orders of the president in his capacity of commander in chief. The Joint Chiefs of Staff, however, remain by law the president's military advisors and, while they normally report through the secretary, they have the specific right to appeal over his head directly to the White House. In addition, there is located in the office of the secretary of defense an assistant secretary for international security affairs, staffed largely by civilian experts and which has occasionally been referred to as "the Pentagon's own State Department."

All of the thousands of people employed by these various departments, agencies, bureaus, and branches are to one degree or another involved with making and carrying out U.S. foreign policy. And the list is actually incomplete; I have omitted discussion of such additional foreign policy influences as the U.S. ambassador to the United Nations, the director of the U.S. Information Agency (both of whom, like the Joint Chiefs of Staff, have the right to deal directly with the president), the Agency for International Development, the Organization of American States, the Military Assistance Program (which operates out of the Pentagon), the Export-Import Bank, and many others. Even departments normally thought of as being of primarily domestic significance get into the act. The Treasury is concerned with international balance of payments problems, the Commerce Department worries about business imports and exports, and so forth.

In the midst of such a labyrinth, it is remarkable that even the president—to whom all involved are ultimately responsible —can obtain the information he needs to formulate rational and timely decisions. For members of the Congress, who share constitutional responsibility for foreign policy, the task is frequently almost impossible.

The Congress affects foreign policy in many ways, some direct and some indirect. Under the Constitution, the House of Representatives is the main revenue raising arm of the government. The ability to appropriate or to withhold funds is obviously a great check on the power of the executive, and was so intended by the writers of the Constitution. The Senate exercises its influence over foreign policy through its ability to withhold consent for the appointment of ambassadors and higher ranking officials of the foreign policy establishment and also, of course, of the defense establishment. The Senate also must give its advice and consent to all treaties by a vote of two-thirds of the senators present. The Senate may give its advice and consent in total, or it may amend the treaty or attach reservations limiting the scope of the treaty. (It is a small technical distinction, perhaps, but it is worth noting that the popular understanding that the Senate must ratify treaties by a two-thirds vote is incorrect. The treaty is actually ratified by the president's signature after the Senate has given its consent in the form of a vote. The significance of the distinction is that while the president cannot ratify a treaty without such a prior vote by the Senate, he is not legally required to ratify any treat which the Senate has approved. He may still decline to sign it, although we in the Senate consider this a ministerial act which he is morally obliged to carry out.)

THE LAG BETWEEN POLICY AND NATIONAL INTERESTS

From this very brief description of the formal mechanisms of foreign policy two things seem obvious. The machine has become so complex that (a) there is now built into the system a multitude of opportunities for oversights and errors, and (b) the constitutional role of the Congress in helping to give direction to foreign policy has been eroded by the complexities of our time.

It has been frequently remarked that "nothing is ever done in Washington until it has needed doing for so long that it's really time to be doing something else." This is nowhere so true as in the operations of foreign policy. To take a hypo-

thetical example, a presidential request to estimate the proba-
bilities of a Communist regime coming to power in Central
America might require months of careful analysis by the appropriate lower level analysts of the State Department, Central
Intelligence Agency, the Defense Department, the National
Security Council and many others. If, as this accumulation of
data about military and political estimates were working its
way up to the President's level, there were to occur a sudden
event such as the Cuban missile crisis, much of the available
analyses would immediately become invalid. The greatest danger, were this to happen, would be that the contingency plans
in being might continue to be used as a basis for policy because those at the top simply failed to realize that they were
actually working from obsolete data, that events had overtaken them.

Something very much like this happened, in fact, during
the Bay of Pigs. Subsequent analysis indicated that the Joint
Chiefs of Staff, in making their projection as to the chances of
success or failure of the invasion plan, assumed a landing at a
particular part of the Cuban coastline. When, for various reasons, a different point was ultimately selected, the original
estimate should have been totally revised—a fact which apparently became clear to no one until after the disaster.

Just as the bureaucratic maze through which foreign policy
decisions now pass, both in the stages of formulation and
implementation, disrupts communications in the executive
branch, so the same factors create a widening gap between
the foreign policy thinking of the executive and the Congress.
Even where there is candor and full disclosure to the appropriate committees of the Congress—which unfortunately has become more the exception than the rule—the intricacies of
policy planning make it hard for the Congress to be sure that
it truly understands the significance of what is being proposed.
Even on the simplest level of appropriating funds, there is
much which the Congress cannot know. Most members of the

Congress, for example, first became aware of the U-2 program when Gary Powers was shot down over Russia, leading Premier Khrushchev to abruptly cancel the proposed summit meeting with President Eisenhower. The entire development and production costs for this expensive aircraft had been successfully camouflaged in the federal budget, so that the true motive of the project was effectively concealed. Similarly, the inflationary problems associated with the war in Vietnam were compounded because the executive branch underestimated the true costs of the war by many billions of dollars.

Finally, under the broad doctrine of executive privilege presently in vogue, responsible members of the Senate Foreign Relations Committee and other bodies of the Congress are frequently denied information not only about current policies but about past policies which were actually arrived at within the executive branch. While there is no single solution, or even a set of solutions, which will completely remedy these communications problems, there are some obvious steps which I believe should be taken.

HOW TO MAKE OUR FOREIGN POLICY MACHINERY MORE FLEXIBLE

As the full story of our involvement in Vietnam unfolds, it becomes apparent that one agency of the executive which has cause to be pleased with its record is the Central Intelligence Agency. It correctly predicted that the bombing of North Vietnam would be unsuccessful and that the will of the North Vietnamese people and government was such that they would not surrender to the type of pressure we intended to apply. It further predicted that the loss of South Vietnam would not mean an automatic Communist takeover in Southeast Asia, with the possible exception of Cambodia. And I believe, incidentally, that this prediction will prove to have been equally accurate.

Unfortunately, these accurate analyses and projections were not acted upon by the ultimate decision makers. One reason, I believe, was the fact that the agency's advice simply got swamped by the kind of contradictory material coming out of the maze of competing intelligence services and groups of analysts in the State and Defense departments and the National Security Council. A second reason, however, is that the CIA was itself involved in operational activities against North Vietnam, and in fact up until mid–1962 it actually had operational control of the army's Green Berets in South Vietnam and Laos. There was a built-in conflict of interests. It is exceedingly difficult for anyone holding responsibility for operations to be objective about the analysis of its intelligence or the results of those operations, actual or potential. If the men who have the responsibility for carrying out operations also have the responsibility for the collection and analysis of intelligence, there is a natural human tendency to shape the intelligence analysis to suit the plans and preconceptions of the operational planners. This is exactly what happened at the Bay of Pigs. We see this constantly, too, with military planners who attempt to evaluate the results of their own planning; air force officials are invariably overoptimistic about the results to be gained from bombing, army officials generally overestimate the effectiveness of infantry in controlling the territory, and the navy is frequently too sanguine about the vulnerability of its ships at sea, as we saw in the Gulf of Tonkin and Pueblo incidents.

Moreover, since this tendency toward wishful thinking is well known, those who evaluate intelligence frequently discount its value in order to make allowance for what they expect to be a built-in bias on the part of the authors.

It is essential, therefore, that the CIA's operations be thoroughly separated from its activities in the collection and collation of intelligence. The co-ordination of intelligence activities was the principal function given to the agency when it was created by the Eightieth Congress and that function has all too frequently been subordinated to other responsibilities.

Secondly, there is a great need for a central intelligence retrieval computer center for the whole government. The phrase "intelligence collection" usually calls to mind visions of James Bond or characters out of books by Eric Ambler. In point of fact, however, intelligence work consists in large measure of the relatively dull process of piecing together many thousands of small scattered bits of information and adding them together until they create a picture. No large picture can emerge today if some of the pieces are in the files of the Defense Intelligence Agency, some in the State Department, some in the FBI, and still others lying around no one knows where. Technology exists today to solve many of these problems. It should be used.

It is theoretically possible, for example, to give the president and his principal advisors in the Defense and State departments small television sets by their bedsides which would give them instant access to whatever intelligence data they might require. Each morning these officials receive the so-called watch reports compiled every night by the Central Intelligence Agency, Defense Intelligence Agency, and the intelligence section of the State Department. At the present time these come to them in the form of a typewritten summary bound into looseleaf notebooks. If they wish to seek greater detail about any item in the report which seems of particular significance they can, of course, telephone the source of the report and ask for further detail. But it has been pointed out that this same material put into computer banks during the night would enable the president, for instance, to simply push a button and have that particular portion of the report revealed on his television tube in greater detail. And by continuing to push the button, he could trace the origin of this particular item down to its minutest detail. Such proposals when made by computer technicians have invariably been resisted by the intelligence community because it amounts to making available raw data, which is a violation of one of the traditional rules of intelligence work. Most intelligence agencies tend to look upon this data much as private business views its competitive trade secrets. This is merely one example of the conditions encountered in modernizing both the organization and the technology of our intelligence machinery. Yet it must be done.

As we streamline our procedure, we must also begin to narrow the gap between the executive and the Congress. One of the great defects of our governmental system in the foreign policy area (and all the others) is that the president and his principal advisors are not formally required to account to anyone for their on-going policies. Once his appointment is confirmed by the Senate, a cabinet officer is accountable only to the president; he cannot be recalled. The president himself is accountable to the voters once every four years; if his policies have varied too greatly from the will of the people they can make known their displeasure by not re-electing him. But four years in the modern world is a very long time.

The simple and effective solution to this problem has long existed and has demonstrated its effectiveness over hundreds of years. It is the formal question hour of the British Parliament. The British prime minister and his Cabinet are required to subject themselves periodically on the floor of the House of Commons to direct questioning by all the members as to their policies and intentions. The nearest institution which we possess in this country is the congressional oversight hearing or the formal press conference, both of which are wholly inadequate. Press conferences are called only at the discretion of the president or his advisors, who also can define arbitrarily the scope of the questioning they will permit. Nor do I believe that the chairman of the Foreign Relations Committee, for example, should have to get his answers about what the executive branch is doing by reading the newspapers.

I believe that as a matter of law we should adopt a requirement that the officers of the cabinet and other senior officers of the executive branch submit themselves to a formal question hour in the legislature on a periodic routine basis. There is nothing radical or experimental about this proposal. As I have said, it has been employed with complete success by our British friends for years. It would not result in any lessening of security for our secrets of state if properly set up—and I believe it would go far toward lessening the continuing credibility gap between our people and their government.

It is time for Congress, as the peoples' representatives, to assert more vigorously their right to know. If the Congress is to act responsibly, then it must have access to the facts. I believe it has a constitutional right to such information, also the power to enforce that right—and a duty to do so.

CHAPTER FIVE

True Long-Term Objectives of American Foreign Policy and How They Should Be Pursued During the Coming Decade

Shortly before the signing of the nuclear test-ban treaty with Russia, which marked the first notable thaw in the cold war, President John F. Kennedy made a memorable speech in Washington. Rejecting the concept of a peace imposed upon the world by either the United States or Russia, he said: "Let us not be blind to our differences, but let us also draw attention to our common interests and the means by which these differences can be resolved. And if we cannot end our differences, at least we can help make the world safe for diversity." Making the world safe for diversity is a far cry from the Great War waged at the beginning of our century to "make the world safe for democracy." If America were to pursue a messianic policy of making the world safe for democracy during the remainder of the century, we would inevitably find ourselves in head-on conflict with the equally messianic policies of other world powers determined to make the world safe for communism. Recognition that we must compromise by accepting the idea of diversity is therefore a great step toward the preservation of world peace.

Those of us who lived through the Second World War emerged from that conflict with the conviction that the overwhelming problem facing mankind was how to avoid a nuclear holocaust and how to build a viable peace in the world. We have succeeded in the first objective for more than a quarter of a century. And while the threat of nuclear disaster still colors all our actions, we can at least say that as for the alcoholic or the drug addict, every day without a drink or a fix is an achievement. Moreover, there is reason to believe that we are moving closer to getting the nuclear monster under control.

No sane person would now contend that the world—or his own messianic cause—could be enhanced through nuclear conflict. The danger, as everyone recognizes, is the possibility of a war which no one wants because of miscalculation. This is precisely what made the war in Vietnam so dangerous. While the conflict stemmed from breaches of faith, breaches which I believe were more flagrant on the part of the United States and of South Vietnam, it escalated as a result of a series of miscalculations by both sides. The North Vietnamese underestimated the willingness of the United States to enter the conflict if necessary to preserve the Saigon regime; the United States grossly underestimated the tenacity and the ability of North Vietnam in prolonging the struggle. Yet, out of that bloody and costly confrontation one encouraging attitude became manifest: The United States, even when its fortunes were at their lowest ebb in Southeast Asia, could act with restraint; it did not resort to nuclear weapons. Using even the smallest of our tactical nuclear weapons we could—as one military leader proposed—have "knocked North Vietnam back to the Stone Age." I regret to say that I have heard the use of these weapons advocated by a responsible American official, although when

I pressed him later in this regard, he said he really meant them to be used in tactical ways to destroy certain areas of the countryside and thus deny passage through those areas to the enemy. I was reminded of the words of the American colonel who was quoted as saying, "To save the village we had to destroy it."

Our reticence may well have been partly the result of realizing that the vacuum we would have created in North Vietnam if nuclear bombing had destroyed Vietnamese power completely would have been quickly filled by China and that a general nuclear war could be the end result.

This lesson has not been lost on our actual or potential adversaries. There are some in our own country who will argue that this reticence will be viewed as an act of weakness and that the danger of war will, therefore, be increased. On the contrary, I believe that we demonstrated in Vietnam that the world's strongest nuclear power—and the only power ever to use nuclear weapons in warfare—is unwilling to resort to them in order to impose its will on a foreign people. By thus reducing apprehension it can only have the effect of lowering international tensions throughout the world.

If we have held back from nuclear destruction, if through mutual limitations on testing and proliferation of nuclear armaments we are successfully cooling down the tensions in our international relations, we are still far from finding a clear formula for constructing a viable peace in the world. This will remain our most pressing problem through the coming decade and thereafter. This is in our national interest and we will have our best chance of achieving it if we pursue that interest with a clear view of our true capabilities.

One way to realize what we can do is to begin by recognizing what we cannot do. For all our wealth and power, we cannot impose a pax americana on the world. We cannot, however laudable our motives, reach out to the ends of the earth to impose our ideas of justice and democracy on peoples who find them strange or unwelcome. At the same time, events in Korea, Vietnam, and Indonesia, as well as the continuing manifestations of nationalism in Czechoslovakia, Poland, Yugoslavia, and the rest of Eastern Europe, have been proving to what former Secretary of State Dean Rusk used to call "the other side" that they can be no more successful in such efforts than ourselves. Thus, there is reason to hope and to believe that the world may be entering what diplomats used to call a "detente" and that the detente may be of long duration, if not permanent.

America actually occupies a position unique in history. Since the first World War we have been the first truly open society which is also the strongest military power of its time. (One might debate whether this was not also true of nineteenth century England, but I would not consider her as truly as open a society as ours in the sense that we use the term here.) History affords many melancholy examples of a democratic society being swallowed up by despotic or totalitarian enemies because of their superior military power. In past conflicts it was the Spartans and the Macedonians who usually carried the day. The real question which faces us is: What should be the foreign policy of an open society which is also richer and more powerful than any potential rivals?

First and foremost, we must recognize that in an open society the conduct of foreign policy is inextricably bound up with public opinion. We saw this in the activities of the peace societies which sprang up following the War of 1812 and we have seen it again most recently and most emphatically in the effects of American public opinion in changing the course of our official policies in Vietnam. The first requirement for a sane and steady foreign policy is a united public.

If we are to have a long peace in the world, manifestly there must be a narrowing of the gap between the haves and the have-not nations. We cannot hope, nor should we, to live forever as a prosperous people in a world where two-thirds of the human race still goes to bed hungry or ill fed at night, if indeed there is a bed to which to go. The underdeveloped nations need foreign aid from the wealthy nations, including especially our own. But no Washington administration will be able to mount a long-range effective program of foreign aid if the residents of ghettos in our own cities, the poor, and the uneducated throughout our America believe that treasure which should be devoted to eliminating their own misery is being sent instead to underprivileged people on the other side of the earth. Similarly, one cannot continue to maintain either our foreign aid programs or even our necessary military defense forces if our own working people and middle class tax payers feel increasingly victimized by runaway inflation and soaring taxes.

Even in the closed Communist societies the leaders have had to take cognizance of such facts. The emphasis on heavy industry and armaments in the Soviet Union, for instance, has had to be toned down because the leadership could no longer ignore mounting policy pressures for a greater number of consumer goods. This is one of the points I so well remember Mr. Kosygin emphasizing in his Kremlin conversation with Senator Gore and me. The same is happening throughout Eastern Europe and will eventually happen in China. The Communists, no less than ourselves, are subject to what Adlai Stevenson called "the revolution of rising expectations."

THE QUANTUM JUMP

While human progress through most of time has followed a gently sloping upward curve, or occasionally leveled off to form centuries-long plateaus during which the life of each new generation was virtually indistinguishable from the one which preceded it, there have been other eras when change came so explosively that attitudes and life styles became obsolete within a single generation. We are in the midst of just such a quantum jump today, and one of greater magnitude than man has previously known. If, as I believe, no nation can pursue a long-term policy in relation to other world powers without a reasonable consensus at home, then American foreign policy for several years to come will depend less upon the calculated plans of professional diplomats than upon the crisis of adjustment among larger segments of our population. The same will be true for the policies of other world powers— and therein lies a considerable danger.

The traumatic effects of this unprecedented rate of change on our domestic institutions—our cities, our schools, our growing unemployment—are all too familiar. Why should we not anticipate equally profound effects on the relations among nations? Right now, for example, despite the best efforts of thousands of scientists and engineers and the expenditure of untold billions of dollars, the United States is less secure than it was twenty-five years ago when the atomic bomb was first developed. So is the Soviet Union. So is Europe. So is China. And if we continue as we are going now—pursuing traditional policies which ignore the facts of life in this new world we have created—then the spending of still more billions will make us less secure ten years from now than we are today.

We speak of the great powers because men have always thought in such terms: Greece and Persia, Rome and Carthage, France and England, Christendom and Islam. But what, today, does it really mean to be a great power? America and Russia, on opposite sides of the world, are within thirty minutes of total mutual destruction if someone decides to push the button. The island of Cuba, thanks to the events of 1962, is free of offensive nuclear weapons—but the episode was a forewarning of the inevitable future. The day will surely come when any small nation can threaten its most powerful neighbor with sufficient destruction to effectively neutralize that neighbor's vastly superior power. We may retain forever the power to erase Cuba from the map—but would we use that force at the certain cost of the destruction of Boston, New York, and Washington? (This possibility is humorously and gently pressed home in Peter Sellers' movie *The Mouse That Roared,* which I believe should be seen by all great power rulers!)

That we need a new calculus for defining national security in this new world is obvious. What is less apparent is our ability to devise it. Today, because of the quantum growth of our knowledge and technological ability, we find ourselves on the threshold of a whole new world. The question is whether we will stumble, perhaps fatally, or whether we can take a deep breath, stand upright, and stride into it.

With 90 percent of all the scientists who have ever lived working today, with the store of human knowledge doubling every ten years, our situation today reminds me of what happened when my Indian forebears met the white man and the so-called blessings of his technologically advanced civilization. Their culture just fell apart. We can see this today on the Indian reservations of the West. The more fortunate Apache may drive to town in a pick-up truck, but it has been bought at the cost of almost everything he and his ancestors cherished —as he will be the first to tell you.

Primitive societies, like our own, are held together by a complex structure of beliefs about the nature of authority and its legitimacy, religion and morality, how man should behave toward one another, the kinds of institutions needed to carry out the functions necessary to maintain the society. The general experience—almost the universal experience—of primitive peoples when confronted by the technological superiority of Western industrial civilization has been the destruction of this whole network of beliefs. Sometimes this happened because Westerners viewed the primitive culture as being in the way; the primitive people and their traditional ways were viewed at best as an inconvenience and at worst as an enemy. They were killed, enslaved, or forcibly converted to Western ways.

In other cases, the primitive peoples participated in the disruption and eventual destruction of their way of life. Cheap manufactured goods of all kinds exerted a powerful pull. It is conventional wisdom, perhaps, to say that this is a good thing. Is not everybody better off with transistor radios, cheap cloth, metal cooking utensils and agricultural tools, firearms and dynamite, motorscooters, and medicine? Perhaps so, but the price paid for these goods by primitive people has been, in many cases, the destruction of their culture.

However the destruction of the primitive social fabric occurred, whether by force or seduction, those individuals who survived were left without cultural moorings. Their old ways —satisfactory under primitive conditions—having been suppressed or discredited, they became a people unable to cope with the new world in which they found themselves. One can see the result today in the squalid, fetid shantytowns in all the major cities of the underdeveloped world. One can see it on many Indian reservations in the United States, where there is a culture of despair and dependency, contributing to abject poverty and horrendous rates of alcoholism and mental illness.

Modern science is the greatest engine of change man has ever known. It is the most effective means of exploring the nature of the universe ever developed. And I am very much afraid our social fabric is no more prepared to face the consequences that will follow than primitive peoples were able to survive their encounter with the West. The only difference is that our own threat comes from within. Suddenly, with cybernetics and automation, we find ourselves facing a future in which a few can produce everything that is needed by all. Men have already visited the moon, and the planets are coming within reach. Here on earth, communication around the globe is almost instantaneous. One can go from one antipode to the other of our world, which is rapidly becoming a world city, or Ecumenopolis, as Constantinos Doxiadis christens it, in almost as little time as an ancient Greek took in walking or even riding from one end to the other of his city-state. The movement of goods and people over vast distances is becoming ever faster and cheaper. When it comes to the ability to kill, nuclear energy has given us the ultimate weapon.

Alas, however, we see now many signs that our moral structure, instead of rising to meet and cope with these challenges, tends to crumble and dissolve.

Production, which should give us the opportunity for leisure, reflection, and rejuvenation of the spirit instead seems to be filling us with restlessness, dissatisfaction and, in some cases, an insatiable greed not seen in the world since the fabled Midas, whose magical touch turned all things to gold— and led to his death by starvation. Television commercials and slick advertising are raising the expectations of all to have what only the few can afford. We find the welfare of individuals sacrificed to the demon of travel, as highways and parking lots gouge through our cities and pave over our landscape. Large areas around major airports are already uninhabitable because of noise and air pollution, and worse is to come. And the quantum increase in our ability to kill has simply been suppressed in our consciousness. We refuse to contemplate what the development of nuclear weapons and the holocaust they make possible really mean. Clausewitz is no longer relevant. War can never again be merely "a pursuit of policy by other means"—unless, of course, the policy is international suicide. And this includes defensive war as well as offensive war, because in a thirty-minute exchange of nuclear destruction, offensive vs. defensive is a distinction without a difference. It won't matter who pushed the first button because there will be no Nuremberg trials after the Third World War. There will be no Nuremberg.

In a world where mankind has acquired the ability to end

history, it is obvious that more is needed than minor modifications of the old diplomacy. Relations among nations must change. Our ways of dealing with one another must be changed, we must revolutionize ourselves. We must match our quantum jump in technology with a quantum jump in social attitudes.

There will be no lasting peace among nations until we succeed in re-establishing equilibrium among men in their daily affairs—an equilibrium which has been the normal condition in most eras of history but which is now singularly lacking. Ironically, we are experiencing this disequilibrium in the first epoch when it is unnecessary. With the acquisition of atomic energy twenty-five years ago, man acquired all the energy he can possibly use. There is no longer any excuse for poverty, deprivation, or fights to death over limited resources. For the first time in man's experience, there is enough for everybody. All that stands in our way is the failure of our culture—of our intelligence—to respond to a world that is wholly new. If we are to survive, we must rid ourselves of the puritan ethos which equates work with virtue—and leisure with vice! We must rid ourselves of another idea which seems deeply rooted in Western thought: that the natural world is an enemy to be subdued and exploited, and, incidentally, destroyed or polluted—and that man is somehow apart from it. We must bring our productive processes under control or they will destroy the earth as certainly as a nuclear war.

We must cease subordinating man to technology. Let us take the future methods of travel and develop them without harming man or hurting the environment. Let us develop a new calculus for weighing the benefits against the costs. The phrase, optimum return, whether used by the government or business, is subject to many interpretations depending on the data we put into the computer. There are too many so-called intangibles—like the sum of human happiness—which are not being cranked in.

We must put a stop to the nuclear arms race by devising a system of international control and supervision over the production and uses of nuclear materials. We must do this because any other course is quite literally insane. But it will take a quantum jump in social awareness to realize it.

According to an official Department of Defense estimate, a hundred and twenty million Americans and a hundred and twenty million Russians would die in an all-out nuclear exchange, within hours. It is difficult to grasp the reality of this figure, but look around, count the ten persons nearest you, imagine six of them dead, and you will begin to get some idea of what nuclear war means. For six of every ten Americans would die. In such a world, the notion of war as merely another form of politics or foreign policy can hardly be called sane.

THEN AND NOW

The objectives of American foreign policy, in the earlier years of our life as a nation have been outlined somewhat as follows:

1. To assure our independence and secure our boundaries.
2. To extend those boundaries to accommodate a growing population and achieve our destiny as a continental power.
3. To safeguard our trading ships on the high seas, assure free access to foreign markets for American commerce, and to protect the interests of our citizens in relation to foreign governments.
4. To preserve our neutrality in relation to foreign wars.
5. To prevent the further colonization of the Western Hemisphere by European or Asian powers.

In all but the fourth of those objectives, we were largely successful. And even in pursuit of the fourth objective, neutrality, we were largely successful in the years between 1776 and 1898, with the single exception of the War of 1812. Not a bad record.

But world events inevitably began to make some of our objectives obsolete and others impossible. As the historian, James A. Garraty, has written about our efforts to remain neutral during the First World War:

Naturally, all the warring nations wanted to draw upon American resources. Under international law, neutrals could trade freely with any belligerent. The Americans were prepared to do so, but because the British fleet dominated the North Atlantic, they could not. Although the specific issues differed somewhat, the situation was similar to that which had prevailed during the Napoleonic Wars. Eager to cut off Germany from foreign products, the British declared nearly all commodities, even foodstuffs, to be contraband of war. They rationed imports to neutral nations such as Denmark and the Netherlands so that they could not transship supplies to Germany. They forced neutral merchantmen into Allied ports in order to search them for goods headed for the enemy. Many cargoes were confiscated, often without payment, and American firms that traded with the Central Powers were "black-listed," which meant that no British subject could deal with them. When these policies caused angry protests in America, the British answered that in a battle for survival they dared not adhere to old-fashioned rules of international law. "If the American shipper grumbles, our reply is that this war is not being conducted for his pleasure or profit," the London *Daily Graphic* explained.

Had the United States insisted that Great Britain abandon these illegal practices, as the Germans demanded, no doubt it could have had its way. It is ironic that an embargo, which failed so ignominiously in Jefferson's day, would have been almost instantly effective if applied at any time after 1914, for American supplies were absolutely vital to the Allies. As the British foreign secretary, Sir Edward Grey, later admitted: "The ill will of the United States meant certain defeat. The object of diplomacy, therefore, was to secure the maximum of blockade that could be enforced without a rupture with the United States."

Although the British tactics frequently exasperated Wilson, he never considered taking such a drastic step. He faced a true dilemma. To allow the British to make the rules meant being unneutral toward the Central Powers. Yet to insist on the old rules, which had never actually been obeyed in wartime, meant being unneutral toward the Allies, for that would have deprived them of much of the value of their naval superiority. *Nothing* the United States might do would be really impartial.

Dante, in his "Inferno," reserved the lowest region of Hell for the souls of those who in life were always neutral. This, at least, is one danger from which we have all escaped: in the complex, interrelated affairs of nations there is no longer a possibility for a truly neutral action; everything we do—or do not do—will affect the course of events, one way or the other. Even the action of not giving military weapons has come, like the mirror in our peculiar Alice in Wonderland world, to be construed as interference in the domestic affairs of another nation. For instance, those of us who have advocated holding up the dispatch of weapons to Greece or Pakistan are accused of interfering in the domestic affairs of those nations.

Our first historical foreign policy objective—to assure our independence as a nation—of course remains. But even here our definition of independence has had to be greatly modified. Our own central bank—The Federal Reserve System—is not even free to regulate our own money supply with regard to the domestic need for more or fewer dollars. It must also carefully consider the consequences of its actions in the international theater; a wrong move could easily create a world-wide financial panic with unforeseeable consequences. In the same vein, the European members of the European Economic Community accept progressive restrictions on their national independence as the price of surviving economically in their peaceful competition with the United States and Japan. Hundreds of other examples—economic, military, and political— could be easily adduced.

Of all the five original foreign policy objectives of our young nation, in fact, only one remains more or less as it was in the beginning: to safeguard the free passage of our ships on the high seas. Yet even here, we are being overtaken by events.

The freedom of the seas has been an axiom of maritime powers throughout the modern era. It was the bedrock of British policy from at least the reign of Elizabeth I and a principal cause of the War of 1812 when England attempted to deny the same freedom to her former colony. But freedom of the seas is rapidly being transformed by contemporary events into what might better be called "the anarchy of ocean space."

THE ANARCHY OF OCEAN SPACE AS AN EXAMPLE OF CRISIS IN FOREIGN POLICY

I have referred earlier to the increasingly frequent crises or confrontations which may be expected among nations as a result of burgeoning technology. New problems are being created in many areas other than the shrinking distances and speeded-up communications to which we alluded in an earlier chapter. One wonders what will happen, for example, when our experiments in weather control eventually give one nation power to pre-empt the available rainfall, to the loss of its neighbors. But this is still in the relatively distant future. The situation of the world's oceans, and the anarchy of ocean space which exists in international law as a heritage from the doctrine of freedom of the seas, is already a critical—though little noticed—problem in the affairs of nations. Nothing better illustrates the impact of technology on foreign policy.

As the world expands its technology in the marine sciences, we are moving toward dangerous legal confrontations with foreign nations over the ownership and jurisdiction of the extraterritorial seabed and the waters above them.

Already we face frequent new problems in the fields of mining, oil well drilling, fisheries, research, and national security in the broad oceans beyond territorial jurisdiction and the continental shelf. The laws of the Sea Conventions of 1958 have brought some definition and legal order to the areas of the continental shelf of each nation. Their weakness is their elastic or nondefinition of the limits of a nation's continental shelf. Bilateral fishing agreements such as those negotiated with the Soviet Union, Japan, and Mexico do bring temporary solutions to certain practical problems as they arise.

My own fear is that, although these case-by-case solutions may be satisfactory for the time being, we might well paint ourselves into the corner in terms of the future national interest and also miss future opportunities for optimum international study and exploration. We stand on the threshold of a vast technological breakthrough which can suddenly advance our nation's (and others') ability to carry out every type of oceanographic activity, at any depth, and in any area of the ocean. To date, there is no adequate mechanism to provide for order when this breakthrough comes.

The United Nations has been conducting a study of the resources of the seas partly with a view to anticipating potential conflict and extending international cooperation. Also in the United Nations, the Intergovernmental Maritime Consultative Organization (to which President Eisenhower honored me by appointing me a member of the original American delegation in 1959) is doing a creditable job trying to resolve *ad hoc* legal problems of the sea that may arise between nations. The Geneva Conventions of 1958 were helpful in dealing with those questions concerning the high seas, the continental shelf, and fisheries which required international action at that time. Nevertheless, despite this useful activity to protect against underocean legal conflict between nations, nothing definitive has really been accomplished.

The agreements with the Soviet Union a few years ago for peaceful use of Antarctica and Outer Space led me to hope that similar action might be undertaken on Inner Space. The problems of the Antarctic and Outer Space differ considerably from those of the oceans, yet the analogy is compelling and the need is more urgent. With the success of these agreements in mind, I drafted a suggested set of principles and a treaty in 1967 in order that our Department of State commence the steps which would lead to an ocean space treaty with all nations for more orderly use of the sea.

When I did this, and at about the same time that Ambassador Pardo of Malta was pressing the same idea in the United Nations, public opinion in America was either skeptical or uninterested in my ideas. I found it difficult to even get witnesses to testify on this subject before the Foreign Relations Committee. Yet, the ideas in my draft set of principles soon came to be accepted. The disarmament aspects were broken out and handled separately, with the result that the Seabed Disarmament Treaty is presently in being. And the remaining portion dealing with the exploration and utilization of the seabeds and the waters above them are the subject of active international negotiation of various United Nations forums. In fact, as a delegate to the Twenty-third General Assembly of the United Nations, I had the honor of pressing the United States position which is very much along the lines of my original set of principles and which is in advance of the views of most other nations, perhaps partly because of my own gentle needling in this regard of our executive branch over a period of several years.

Today, we find that the area most susceptible to adoption of such a treaty is the extraterritorial seabed and the resources under the bottom of the world ocean. There is another area however which presents a potential of more difficult legal snarls: the high seas themselves and the natural resources they contain.

Soon we must attend to the inevitable problems that we may expect as undersea technology continues to expand at a near geometric progression. I am thinking specifically of the jurisdictional and ownership considerations that must intrude into the development of aquaculture, fish husbandry, undersea research, scientific preserves, sport areas, undersea tourism, and many other activities now only dreamed of but sure to occur before long. The time will soon come when, instead of hunting fish, we will farm them, much as the European settlers brought animal husbandry to America in lieu of hunting as practiced by the Indians or early European explorers. As history has shown, a visionary Jules Verne today can foretell fantastic but real accomplishments of tomorrow—just as Jules Verne predicted the globe-circling nuclear submarine, "Nautilus."

It is difficult to fix the exact limits for the legally defined continental shelf. Which of us is in a position to know all the economic, technologic, political, and other factors relating to any proposal for establishing a fixed limit—factors which caused so much debate and concern at the 1958 Geneva Conference? These and other problems of the extraterritorial seas must nevertheless be brought under the discipline of a reasonable legal pattern if we are to avoid hopelessly complex confrontations in the near future. The first step should be greater knowledge and broader international understanding through exploration of the ocean floor.

But even these pressing considerations seem legalistic and out-of-date in comparison to the problem of oceanic pollution. The entire Southern Atlantic from Africa to Brazil is now afloat with the debris of modern civilization. Garbage dumped into the Pacific off the coast of California shows up on the shores of Japan. When an archeologist skin diver recently swam to the floor of the Mediterranean, the first sight to greet his eyes was not an ancient Greek temple or statue, but a page from the newspaper, *Le Figaro*.

In an earlier chapter, I suggested that time is a fourth dimension which must be considered in the conduct of foreign policy. This is true in the context of rival political ideologies, but there are other threats to the survival of humanity than the conflicts growing out of political ideologies and national ambition. And in these areas, patience will not be enough, for time is against us. The oceans and the atmosphere are common possessions of all mankind—and we are rapidly destroying them. The earth's resources are dwindling at an ever-increasing pace. World population continues to grow—and two-thirds of that population is already underfed. The earth's present population of 3.7 billion people will reach 7 billion by the year 2000. In order to merely maintain our present levels of inadequate nutrition, we will have to at least double world-wide food production in three decades. No nation can do this alone; it requires universal effort. Yet our principal foreign policy concern in the area of agriculture today—on the part of all countries—is how to keep foreign agricultural surpluses from depressing domestic prices for farmers.

This has been, all along, the major stumbling block for the common market countries in coordinating their economics, and is today the principal dispute between the United States and the European Economic Community because of the latter's high tariffs against the importation of American farm products. In a world teetering on the brink of starvation, this borders on racial insanity.

No one nation can solve the problem of how to give the human race enough to eat.

No one nation can stop the poisoning of the oceans—70 percent of the earth's surface.

No one nation can prevent the pollution of the air which all of us must breathe.

Recognition of the fact that communists and capitalists alike breathe the same air was probably the decisive element in bringing about the nuclear test ban agreement—ignored, however, by France and China because the leaders of both countries, their eyes fixed on the "political realities" of the past, were incapable of realizing that we are living in a new world.

The lag between national interest and foreign policy is not confined to the United States: it is now a problem for all nations because we are still trying to play the historic game of nations when most of the old rules have become at best irrelevant and at worst a certain path to disaster.

Aldous Huxley once remarked that most of the human race goes to bed hungry every night. Therefore, we may conclude that until such time as the question, How can we get people enough to eat? leads the agenda of every international conference, our statesmen do not truly represent the interests of the bulk of the people.

I believe, in short, that the age of political ideology and bilateral confrontation is past. The true course of international diplomacy is to direct itself to the overriding problems created by the world's multiplying population and the starvation, deprivation, and world-wide pollution of the environment which goes with it. The quantum jump in technology, and in the sheer number of human beings sharing the same planet, has in our lifetime overturned virtually all the old philosophies for the conduct of affairs among nations. If we are to survive, we must recognize that it will make no difference whether the last man to survive on an uninhabited planet happens to be a communist or a capitalist.

We must bear in mind Palmerston's dictum that national policies must reflect true national interests—and that, as interests change, so must policies. If policies are carried on unchanged while interests change, we find ourselves in increasingly unrealistic positions, which is just where we find ourselves in Vietnam and in so many other parts of the world.

We must bear in mind that international agreements, in

order to last, must be of mutual advantage, must be voluntary, and must contain sanctions sufficiently severe to ensure a better chance of their not being broken.

We must bear in mind the interdependence of all the world's people, an interdependence that increases with the raising of the technology of the various nations.

We must bear in mind that the greatest natural resource is technological ability and education. As Jean-Jacques Servan-Schreiber puts it, "The one really important natural resource is gray matter."

We must bear in mind that, while technology and the means of production, of travel and of communication, and of war and destruction are enlarging at a geometric rate, human nature and desires are constant. Man today is drawn by pretty much the same basic desires as he was two thousand years ago. And these desires are pretty much the same throughout our world. That is why true communism, which runs against so many of man's basic desires, contains the seeds of its own destruction within itself.

We must realize that the real interest of all nations is now essentially the same, and that politics and ideologies are in our era essentially irrelevant. Communists and capitalists have different definitions of freedom. But we are going to have to accept the fact that before one can be free by any definition, one must first be alive. And the desirability of human survival is surely something upon which we can all agree.

We can not decide for other nations; we can only hope. But for ourselves, we can determine that America's voice in the world will be raised on behalf of the real problems of the last third of the twentieth century and not used in querrulous debate and continuous conflict with the ghosts of people who never saw an airplane or envisioned a world where two powerful nations on opposite sides of the globe could in half an hour obliterate the human race.

Our technical problems can be met, but not without quantum jumps still to be made in our thinking. Peace is the single most important problem confronting us. But a nation's foreign policy grows out of its own internal situation and men cannot be at peace with their neighbors unless they are at peace with themselves. It is quite true that there are many people in the world who do not wish us well, and it is also true that there are a few citizens of our own country who feel the same way. The gravest threat to our well being, however, comes not from outside or from any international or even internal conspiracy, but from ourselves, those of us whose ideas and ways of life fall within the mainstream of American society. As inheritors of the New World, we are still the last best hope of mankind. If we cannot make the changes in our institutions and ways of thought that are required to cope with change, no one will do it for us. We will have the thanks of our descendents if we succeed. If we fail, we may not have descendents.

Appendix

In the foregoing pages I have suggested more than once that the pendulum of power in the conduct of foreign policy has swung too far toward the executive branch of the government. One of the required corrective actions, I believe, is for the Congress to reassert its constitutional prerogatives and to show greater initiative. This is precisely what I attempted to do with respect to the treaty on the use of ocean space, acting in my capacity as chairman of the Subcommittee on Ocean Space of the Committee on Foreign Relations.

In pursuing this objective, we reversed the normal procedure. Instead of awaiting a treaty proposal by the White House and the State Department, my staff and I formulated a set of legal principles which we felt should govern the activities of nations in the international marine environment. Subsequently, after extensive hearings before the committee, we embodied those principles in a draft treaty which was laid before the Senate and the Committee on Foreign Relations. In a sense, this was our method for pressing the executive branch to take action and to consider the problem in greater depth than would otherwise be the case. The results, I think, are evident in the two documents which comprise this appendix. The first—the result of our labors in the Senate—is Senate Resolution Number 92, which is our proposal of a model treaty to the executive branch. The second document is the treaty formally proposed by the government of the United States to the United Nations. It is, in my opinion, a far better document than would have existed had we in the Senate not taken the initiative.

I have appended both of these documents not merely because of the enormous importance which I attach to international negotiations on the subject of ocean space, but also because I think this approach of congressional initiative in the generation and promulgation of treaties should become the rule rather than the exception.

This is an area in which the people's representatives have the right to propose, as well as dispose, and we can do much to re-establish the equilibrium of our constitutional checks-and-balances by exercising this right—which is in reality not only a right but an obligation.

SENATE RESOLUTION 92

Relative to Ocean Space Treaty

91 Congress   1st Session

In the Senate of the United States

FEBRUARY 4, 1969

Mr. PELL submitted the following resolution; which was referred to the Committee on Foreign Relations

RESOLUTION

Whereas the threat of anarchy is imminent in the field of scientific exploration and commercial exploitation of the deep sea and its resources; and

Whereas international agreement on a rule of law governing the activities of nations in the exploration and exploitation of the deep sea and its resources is in the common interest of all mankind: Now, therefore, be it

Resolved, That it is the sense of the Senate that the President should take all necessary steps, through the Secretary of State, the United States delegation to the United Nations, or any other appropriate agency or officer of the United States, to enter into negotiations with representatives of the governments of the major coastal and maritime nations and all other interested nations of the world to the end that there shall be concluded, with as widespread acceptance as is possible, a treaty on the peaceful exploration and exploitation of ocean space as follows:

TREATY ON PRINCIPLES GOVERNING THE ACTIVITIES OF STATES IN THE EXPLORATION AND EXPLOITATION OF OCEAN SPACE

PREAMBLE

The States Parties to this Treaty,

Inspired by the great prospects opening up before mankind as a result of man's ever-deepening probe of ocean space—the waters of the high seas, including the superjacent waters above the continental shelf and outside the territorial sea of each nation, and the seabed and subsoil of the submarine areas of the high seas outside the area of the territorial sea and continental shelf of each nation,

Recognizing the common heritage of mankind in ocean space and the common interest of all mankind in the exploration of ocean space and the exploitation of its resources for peaceful purposes,

Believing that the threat of anarchy exists in the exploration and exploitation of ocean space and its resources,

Desiring to contribute to broad international cooperation in the scientific as well as the legal aspects of the exploration and exploitation of ocean space and its resources for peaceful purposes,

Recalling the four conventions on the Law of the Sea and an optional protocol of signature concerning the compulsory settlement of disputes, which agreements were formulated at the United Nations Conference on the Law of the Sea, held at Geneva from 24 February to 27 April 1958, and were adopted by the Conference at Geneva on 29 April 1958,

Recalling the Treaty on Principles Governing the Activities of States in the Exploration and Use of Outer Space, Including the Moon and Other Celestial Bodies, which was unanimously endorsed by United Nations General Assembly resolution 2222 (XXI) of 19 December 1966 and signed by sixty nations at Washington, London, and Moscow on 27 January 1967, and considering that progress towards international cooperation in the exploration and exploitation of ocean space and its resources and the development of the rule of law in this area of human endeavor is of comparable importance to that achieved in the field of outer space,

Recalling United Nations General Assembly resolution 2467A of 21 December 1968, which provided for the establishment of a Committee on the Peaceful Uses of the Seabed and Ocean Floor Beyond the Limits of National Jurisdiction, and the uses of their resources in the interests of mankind,

Recognizing that the problems resulting from the commercial exploitation of ocean space are imminent,

Believing that the living and mineral resources in suspension in the high seas, and in the seabed and subsoil of ocean space, are free for the use of all nations, subject to international treaty obligations and the conservation provisions of the four conventions on the Law of the Sea,

Convinced that a Treaty on Principles Governing the Activities of States in the Exploration and Exploitation of Ocean Space will further the welfare and prosperity of mankind and benefit their national States,

Have agreed as follows:

PART I
GENERAL PRINCIPLES APPLICABLE TO OCEAN SPACE

ARTICLE 1
The exploration and use of ocean space and the resources in ocean space shall be carried out for the benefit and in the interests of all mankind, and shall be the province of all mankind.

ARTICLE 2
Ocean space and the resources in ocean space shall be free for exploration and exploitation by all nations without discrimination of any kind, on a basis of equality of opportunity, and in accordance with international law, and there shall be free access to all areas of ocean space.

ARTICLE 3
Ocean space is not subject to national appropriation by claim of sovereignty, by means of use of occupation, or by any other means.

ARTICLE 4
There shall be freedom of scientific investigation in ocean space and States Parties to the Treaty shall facilitate and encourage international cooperation in such investigation, but no acts or activities taking place pursuant to such investigation shall constitute a basis for asserting or creating any right to exploration or exploitation of ocean space and its resources.

ARTICLE 5
States Parties to the Treaty shall carry on activities in the exploration and exploitation of ocean space and its resources in accordance with international law, including the Charter of the United Nations, and the provisions contained in these articles, in the interest of maintaining international peace and security and promoting international cooperation and understanding.

ARTICLE 6

States Parties to the Treaty shall bear international responsibility for national activities in ocean space, whether carried on by governmental agencies or nongovernmental entities or nationals of such States, and for assuring that national activities are carried on in conformity with the provisions set forth in this Treaty. The activities of nongovernmental entities and nationals of States in ocean space shall require authorization and continuing supervision by the appropriate State Party to the Treaty. When activities are carried on in ocean space by an international organization, responsibility for compliance with this Treaty shall be borne by the international organization itself.

ARTICLE 7

In the exploration of ocean space and the exploitation of its resources, States Parties to the Treaty shall be guided by the principle of cooperation and mutual assistance and shall conduct all their activities in ocean space with due regard for the corresponding interests of all other States Parties.

ARTICLE 8

States Parties to the Treaty shall render all possible assistance to any person, vessel, vehicle, or facility found in ocean space in danger of being lost or otherwise in distress.

ARTICLE 9

States Parties to the Treaty engaged in activities of exploration or exploitation in ocean space shall immediately inform the other States Parties or the Secretary General of the United Nations of any phenomena they discover in ocean space which could constitute a danger to the life or health of persons exploring or working in ocean space.

PART II
USE OF OCEAN SPACE EXCEPT SEABED AND SUBSOIL

ARTICLE 10

All States Parties to the Treaty shall have the right for their nationals to engage in fishing, aquaculture, insolution mining, transportation, and telecommunication in the waters of ocean space beyond the territorial seas of any State.

ARTICLE 11

The right declared in Article 10 shall be subject to the treaty obligations of each State Party to the Treaty and to the interests and rights of coastal States and shall be conditioned upon fulfillment of the conservation measures required in the agreement entitled 'Convention on Fishing and Conservation of the Living Resources of the High Seas,' adopted by the United Nations Conference on the Law of the Sea at Geneva on 29 April 1958.

ARTICLE 12

Any disputes which may arise between States Parties to the Treaty with respect to fishing, aquaculture, insolution mining, conservation, and transportation activities in the high seas shall be settled in accordance with all the provisions of the convention referred to in Article 11 setting forth a compulsory method for the settlement of such questions. The provisions of Article 27 and Annex 4 of the International Telecommunication Convention, signed at Geneva on December 21, 1959, shall be applicable to any disputes which may arise between States Parties with respect to telecommunication activities in the high seas.

PART III
USE OF SEABED AND SUBSOIL OF OCEAN SPACE

ARTICLE 13

In order to promote and maintain international cooperation in the peaceful and orderly exploration, and exploitation of the natural resources, of the seabed and subsoil of submarine areas of ocean space, each State Party to the Treaty undertakes to engage in such exploration or exploitation only under licenses issued by a technically competent licensing authority to be designated by the United Nations and to be independent of any State.

ARTICLE 14

The natural resources referred to in this Part consist of the mineral and other nonliving resources of the seabed and subsoil together with living organisms belonging to sedentary species, that is to say, organisms which, at the harvestable stage, either are immobile on or under the seabed or are unable to move except in constant physical contact with the seabed or the subsoil.

ARTICLE 15

The activities of nationals and nongovernmental entities in the exploration of submarine areas of ocean space and the exploitation of the natural resources of such areas shall require authorization and continuing supervision by the appropriate State Party to the Treaty, and shall be conducted under licenses issued to States Parties to the Treaty making application on behalf of their nationals and nongovernmental entities. When such activities are to be carried on by an international organization, a license may be issued to such organization as if it were a State.

ARTICLE 16

It shall be the duty of the licensing authority referred to in Article 13 to act as promptly as possible on each application for a license made to it. In issuing licenses and prescribing regulations, the licensing authority shall apply all relevant provisions set forth in this Treaty, shall give due consideration to the potential impact on the world market for each resource to be extracted or produced under such license, and shall apply the following criteria:

(a) The license issued by the licensing authority shall (i) cover an area of such size and dimensions as the licensing authority may determine, with due regard given to providing for a satisfactory return of investment, (ii) be for a period of not more than fifty years, with the option of renewal, provided that operations are conducted with the approval of the licensing authority, (iii) require the payment to the licensing authority of such fee or royalty as may be specified in the lease, (iv) require that such lease will terminate within a period of not more than ten years in the absence of operations thereunder unless the licensing authority approves an extension of the period of such license, and (v) contain such other reasonable requirements as the licensing authority may deem necessary to implement the provisions of this Treaty and to provide for the most efficient exploitation of resources possible, consistent with the conservation of and prevention of the waste of the natural resources of the seabed and subsoil of ocean space.

(b) If two or more States Parties to the Treaty apply for licenses to engage in the exploration of the seabed and subsoil of ocean space or the exploitation of its natural resources in the same area or areas of ocean space, the licensing authority shall, to the greatest extent feasible and practicable, encourage cooperative or joint working relations between such States, and be guided by the principle that ocean space shall be free for use by all States, without discrimination of any kind, on a basis of equality of opportunity. But, if it proves impractical for the license to be shared, the licensing authority shall determine which State Party to the Treaty shall receive the license with due regard given to the encouragement of the development of the technologically developing States.

(c) A coastal State has a special interest in the conservation of the natural resources of the seabed and subsoil of ocean space adjacent to its territorial sea and continental shelf and this interest shall be taken into account by the licensing authority.

(d) A coastal State is entitled to take part on an equal footing in any system of research and regulation for purposes of conservation of the natural resources of the seabed and subsoil of ocean space in that area, even though its agencies or nationals do not engage in exploration there or exploitation of its natural resources.

(e) The exploration of the seabed and subsoil of ocean space and the exploitation of its natural resources must not result in any un-justifiable interference with navigation, fishing, or the conservation of the living resources of the sea, nor result in any interference with fundamental oceanographic or other scientific research carried out with the intention of open publication.

(f) A State or international organization holding a license is obliged to undertake, in the area covered by such license, all appropriate measures for the protection of the living resources of the sea from harmful agents and shall pursue its activities so as to avoid the harmful contamination of the environment of such area.

ARTICLE 17

1. Subject to appropriate regulations prescribed by the licensing authority referred to in Article 13 and to the following provisions, a State or international organization holding a license shall be entitled to construct and maintain or operate on the seabed and subsoil of ocean space installations and other devices necessary for its exploration and the exploitation of its natural resources, and to establish safety zones around such installations and devices and to take in those zones measures necessary for their protection.

2. The safety zones referred to in this Article may extend to a distance of 500 meters radius around the installations and other devices which have been erected, measured from each point of their outer edge. Ships of all nationalities must respect these safety zones.

3. Such installations and devices do not possess the status of islands and have no territorial sea of their own.

4. Due notice must be given of the construction of any such installations, and permanent means for giving warning of their presence must be maintained. Any installations which are abandoned or disused must be entirely removed by the State or international organization responsible for its construction.

5. Neither the installations or devices, nor the safety zones around them, may be established where interference may be caused to the use of recognized sea lanes essential to international commerce and navigation.

ARTICLE 18

To the greatest extent feasible and practicable, the licensing authority referred to in Article 13 shall disseminate immediately and effectively information and data received by it from license owners regarding their activities in ocean space.

ARTICLE 19

If a State Party to the Treaty has reason to believe that an activity or experiment planned by it or its nationals or nongovernmental entities under a license issued pursuant to this Part would cause potentially harmful interference with activities of other States Parties in the peaceful exploration and exploitation of ocean space, it shall undertake appropriate international consultations and obtain the consent of the licensing authority referred to in Article 13 before proceeding with such activity or experiment. A State Party to the Treaty which has reason to believe that an activity or experiment planned by another State Party would cause potentially harmful interference with activities in the peaceful exploration and exploitation of submarine areas of ocean space may request consultation concerning the activity or experiment and submit a request for consideration of its complaint to the licensing authority, which may order that the activity or experiment shall be suspended, modified, or prohibited. Review of any such order shall be allowed in accordance with the provisions of Article 24.

ARTICLE 20

All stations, installations, equipment, and sea vehicles, machines, and capsules used on the seabed or in the subsoil of ocean space, whether manned or unmanned, shall be open to representatives of the licensing authority referred to in Article 13, except that if there is objection to this procedure by the licensee, such facilities shall be open only to the Sea Guard of the United Nations as set forth in Article 27 of this Treaty.

ARTICLE 21

Whenever a State Party to the Treaty or an international organization fails to comply with any of the provisions of a license issued to it under this Part, such license may be canceled by the licensing authority referred to in Article 13, upon thirty days notice to the State or international organization concerned, but subject to the right of the license owner to correct any failure of compliance within a reasonable period of time to be specified by the licensing authority, and, in any event, to request review of the decision of the licensing authority as set forth in Article 24.

ARTICLE 22

Any dispute which may arise under this Part between States or international organizations holding licenses, or between license owners and the licensing authority referred to in Article 13, shall first be submitted for settlement by the licensing authority which shall determine its own procedure, assuring each party a full opportunity to be heard and to present its case.

ARTICLE 23

In all cases of disputes under this Part, whether among license owners or between license owners and the licensing authority referred to in Article 13, the licensing authority shall be empowered to make awards.

ARTICLE 24

1. In the case of any dispute under this Part, if the licensing authority shall not have rendered its decision within a reasonable period of time or if any party to a dispute under this Part desires review of the decision of the licensing authority, such dispute shall, at the request of any of the parties, be submitted to a standing review panel which shall consist of not more than three members to be

appointed by the International Court of Justice. The decision of the licensing authority shall be final and binding upon all parties to a proceeding before it unless a request for a review of such decision is made under this Article within a period of thirty days from receipt by such parties of notice of such decision.

2. No two members of the panel may be nationals of the same State. No member may participate in the decision of any case if he has previously taken part in such case in any capacity or if he is a national of any party involved in the case.

3. Members of the panel shall serve at the pleasure of the International Court of Justice. The Court shall fix the salaries, allowances, and compensation of members of the panel. The expenses of the panel shall be borne by each party to proceedings before the panel in such a manner as shall be decided by the Court.

4. The panel shall determine its own procedure, assuring each party to the proceeding a full opportunity to be heard and to present its case.

5. The panel shall hear and determine each case within a period of ninety days from receipt of a request for review of such case, unless it decides, in case of necessity, to extend the time limit for a period not exceeding thirty additional days. The decision of the panel shall be by majority vote and shall be final and binding upon the parties to the proceeding; except that if any party to the proceeding desires review of the decision, or if the panel has failed to render its decision within the period prescribed in the preceding sentence, the case shall be within the compulsory jurisdiction of the International Court of Justice as contemplated by paragraph 1 of Article 36 of the Statute of the International Court of Justice, and may accordingly be brought before the Court by an application made by such party.

PART IV

USE OF SEABED AND SUBSOIL OF OCEAN SPACE FOR PEACEFUL PURPOSES ONLY

ARTICLE 25

1. The seabed and subsoil of submarine areas of ocean space shall be used for peaceful purposes only.

2. The prohibitions of this Part shall not be construed to prevent—

(A) the use of military personnel or equipment for scientific research or for any other peaceful purpose;

(B) the temporary use or stationing of any military submarines on the seabed or subsoil of ocean space if such submarines are not primarily designed or intended for use or stationing on the seabed or subsoil of ocean space; or

(C) the use or stationing of any device on or in the seabed or subsoil of ocean space which is designed and intended for purposes of submarine or weapons detection, identification, or tracking.

ARTICLE 26

1. Each of the States Parties to this Treaty undertakes to refrain from the implacement or installation on or in the seabed or subsoil of ocean space of any objects containing nuclear weapons or any kinds of weapons of mass destruction, or the stationing of such weapons on or in the seabed or subsoil of ocean space in any other manner.

2. Each of the States Parties to this Treaty undertakes furthermore to refrain from causing, encouraging, or in any way participating in the conduct of the activities described in paragraph 1 of this Article.

ARTICLE 27

All stations, installations, equipment, and sea vehicles, machines, and capsules, whether manned or unmanned, on the seabed or in the subsoil of ocean space shall be open to representatives of other States Parties to the Treaty on a basis of reciprocity, but only with the consent of the State concerned. Such representatives shall give reasonable advance notice of a projected visit in order that appropriate consultations may be held and that maximum precautions may be taken to assure safety and to avoid interference with normal operations in the facility to be visited. All such facilities shall be open at any time to the Sea Guard of the United Nations referred to in Part VII of this Treaty, subject to the control of the Security Council as set forth in such Part.

PART V
REGULATIONS ON THE DISPOSAL OF RADIOACTIVE WASTE MATERIAL IN OCEAN SPACE

ARTICLE 28

The disposal of radioactive waste material in ocean space shall be subject to safety regulations to be prescribed by the International Atomic Energy Agency, in consultation with the licensing authority referred to in Article 13 of this Treaty.

ARTICLE 29

In the event of the conclusion of any other international agreements concerning the use of nuclear energy, including the disposal
of radioactive waste material, to which all of the States Parties to the
Treaty are parties, the rules established under such agreements shall
apply in ocean space.

PART VI
LIMITS OF CONTINENTAL SHELF

ARTICLE 30

In order to assure freedom of the exploration and exploitation of
ocean space and its resources as provided in this Treaty, there is a
clear necessity that fixed limits must be set for defining the outer
boundaries of the continental shelf of coastal States. For the purpose
of the provisions of this Treaty, the term "continental shelf" is used
as referring (a) to the seabed and subsoil of the submarine areas
adjacent to the coast but outside the area of the territorial sea to a
depth of 550 meters, or to a distance of 50 miles from the baselines
from which the breadth of the territorial sea is measured, whichever
results in the greatest area of continental shelf, and (b) to the seabed
and subsoil of similar submarine areas adjacent to the coasts of islands. In no case, however, shall the continental shelf be considered
for such purpose to encompass an area greater than the area (exclusive of territorial sea) of the State or island to which it is adjacent.
Recognizing the desirability of achieving agreement on unsettled
questions relating to defining the boundaries of the continental shelf,
States Parties to the Treaty undertake to accept any agreements which
may be reached in the event a conference is convened to consider
such questions as provided for in Article 13 of the Convention on
the Continental Shelf, adopted at Geneva on 29 April 1958; and any
agreement so reached shall become effective for purposes of this
Treaty when approved by the conference.

PART VII
SEA GUARD

ARTICLE 31

In order to promote the objectives and ensure the observance of
the provisions set forth in this Treaty, States Parties to the Treaty
agree that there shall be established as a permanent force a Sea Guard

of the United Nations which may take such action as may be necessary to maintain and enforce international compliance with these
principles.

ARTICLE 32

The Sea Guard shall be under the control of the Security Council
of the United Nations, in consultation with the licensing authority
referred to in Article 13 of this Treaty. Paragraph 3 of Article 27
of the Charter of the United Nations shall be applicable to decisions
of the Security Council made with respect to the Sea Guard. The
licensing authority shall be responsible under the Security Council
for the supervision of the Sea Guard in connection with the performance by the Sea Guard of such duties as the licensing authority may
deem appropriate to assign or delegate to the Sea Guard for purposes
of the implementation of Part III of this Treaty.

ARTICLE 33

States Parties to the Treaty are encouraged to provide to the Sea
Guard such personnel and suitable scientific and sea patrol vessels
as are necessary for the establishment and maintenance of the Sea
Guard.

PART VIII
NATIONAL LAWS TO APPLY TO CRIMES IN OCEAN
SPACE PENDING INTERNATIONAL AGREEMENT
ON CODE OF CRIMINAL LAW

ARTICLE 34

Pending agreement upon an international code of law governing
criminal activities in ocean space and the institution of an appropriate tribunal with jurisdiction over violations of such code of law,
personnel of States Parties to the Treaty and nongovernmental entities of State Parties and international organizations engaged in activities of exploration or exploitation in ocean space shall be subject
only to the jurisdiction of the State of which they are nationals or
the State which bears responsibility for their activities in respect of
all acts or omissions occurring while they are in ocean space, unless
otherwise provided for by international law or in this Treaty.

PART IX
FINAL ARTICLES

ARTICLE 35

1. The provisions of this Treaty shall apply to the activities of States Parties to the Treaty in the exploration and exploitation of ocean space, whether such activities are carried on by a single State Party to the Treaty or jointly with other States, including cases where they are carried on within the framework of international intergovernmental organizations.

2. Any practical questions arising in connection with activities carried on by international intergovernmental organizations in the exploration and exploitation of ocean space, shall be resolved by the States Parties to the Treaty either with the appropriate international organization or with one or more States members of that international organization, which are Parties to this Treaty.

ARTICLE 36

1. This Treaty shall be open to all States for signature. Any State which does not sign this Treaty before its entry into force in accordance with paragraph 3 of this Article may accede to it at any time.

2. This Treaty shall be subject to ratification by signatory States. Instruments of ratification and instruments of accession shall be deposited with the Governments of the United States of America, the United Kingdom of Great Britain and Northern Ireland, and the Union of Soviet Socialist Republics, which are hereby designated the Depositary Governments.

3. This Treaty shall enter into force upon the deposit of instruments of ratification by ten Governments including the Governments designated as Depositary Governments under this Treaty.

4. For States whose instruments of ratification or accession are deposited subsequent to the entry into force of this Treaty, it shall enter into force on the date of the deposit of their instruments of ratification or accession.

5. The Depositary Governments shall promptly inform all signatory and acceding States of the date of each signature, the date of deposit of each instrument of ratification of and accession to this Treaty, the date of its entry into force and other notices.

6. This Treaty shall be registered by the Depositary Governments pursuant to Article 102 of the Charter of the United Nations.

ARTICLE 37

Any State Party to the Treaty may propose amendments to this Treaty. Amendments shall enter into force for each State Party to the Treaty accepting the amendments upon their acceptance by a majority of the States Parties to the Treaty and thereafter for each remaining State Party to the Treaty on the date of acceptance by it.

ARTICLE 38

Any State Party to the Treaty may give notice of its withdrawal from the Treaty one year after its entry into force by written notification to the Depositary Governments. Such withdrawal shall take effect one year from the date of receipt of this notification.

ARTICLE 39

This Treaty, of which the English, Russian, French, Spanish, Chinese, and Arabic texts are equally authentic, shall be deposited in the archives of the Depositary Governments. Duly certified copies of this Treaty shall be transmitted by the Depositary Governments to the Governments of the signatory and acceding States.

IN WITNESS WHEREOF the undersigned, duly authorized, have signed this Treaty.

DONE in triplicate, at the capital cities of the Depositary Governments at Washington, Moscow, and London, this _____ day of _____ one thousand nine hundred and _____.

For the United States of America:

For the Union of Soviet Socialist Republics:

For the United Kingdom of Great Britain and Northern Ireland:

*Committee on the Peaceful Uses of the Seabed and the Ocean Floor
Beyond the Limits of National Jurisdiction*

DRAFT UNITED NATIONS CONVENTION ON THE INTERNATIONAL SEABED AREA

Working Paper

The attached draft of a United Nations Convention on the International Seabed Area is submitted by the United States Government as a working paper for discussion purposes.

The draft Convention and its Appendices raise a number of questions with respect to which further detailed study is clearly necessary and do not necessarily represent the definitive views of the United States Government. The Appendices in particular are included solely by way of example.

UNITED NATIONS CONVENTION ON THE INTERNATIONAL SEABED AREA

CHAPTER I
BASIC PRINCIPLES

ARTICLE 1

1. The International Seabed Area shall be the common heritage of all mankind.

2. The International Seabed Area shall comprise all areas of the seabed and subsoil of the high seas [1] seaward of the 200 meter isobath adjacent to the coast of continents and islands.

3. Each Contracting Party shall permanently delineate the precise boundary of the International Seabed Area off its coast by straight lines not exceeding 60 nautical miles in length, following the general direction of the limit specified in paragraph 2. Such lines shall connect fixed points at the limit specified in paragraph 2, defined permanently by co-ordinates of latitude and longitude. Areas between or landward of such points may be deeper than 200 meters. Where a trench or trough deeper than 200 meters transects an area less than 200 meters in depth, a straight boundary line more than 60 nautical

[1] *Note:* The United States has simultaneously proposed an international Convention which would, *inter alia,* fix the boundary between the territorial sea and the high seas at a maximum distance of twelve nautical miles from the coast.

miles in length, but not exceeding the lesser of one fourth of the length of that part of trench or trough transecting the area 200 meters in depth or 120 nautical miles, may be drawn across the trench or trough.

4. Each Contracting Party shall submit the description of the boundary to the International Seabed Boundary Review Commission within five years of the entry into force of this Convention for such Contracting Party. Boundaries not accepted by the Commission and not resolved by negotiation between the Commission and the Contracting Party within one year shall be submitted by the Commission to the Tribunal in accordance with Section E of Chapter IV.

5. Nothing in this Article shall affect any agreement or prejudice the position of any Contracting Party with respect to the delimitation of boundaries between opposite or adjacent States in seabed areas landward of the International Seabed Area, or with respect to any delimitation pursuant to Article 30.

ARTICLE 2

1. No State may claim or exercise sovereignty or sovereign rights over any part of the International Seabed Area or its resources. Each Contracting Party agrees not to recognize any such claim or exercise of sovereignty or sovereign rights.

2. No State has, nor may it acquire, any right, title, or interest in the International Seabed Area or its resources except as provided in this Convention. (The preceding Article is not intended to imply that States do not currently have rights under, or consistent with, the 1958 Geneva Convention on the Continental Shelf.)

ARTICLE 3

The International Seabed Area shall be open to use by all States, without discrimination, except as otherwise provided in this Convention.

ARTICLE 4

The International Seabed Area shall be reserved exclusively for peaceful purposes.

ARTICLE 5

1. The International Seabed Resource Authority shall use revenues it derives from the exploration and exploitation of the mineral resources of the International Seabed Area for the benefit of all mankind, particularly to promote the economic advancement of de-

veloping States Parties to this Convention, irrespective of their geographic location. Payments to the Authority shall be established at levels designed to ensure that they make a continuing and substantial contribution to such economic advancement, bearing in mind the need to encourage investment in exploration and exploitation and to foster efficient development of mineral resources.

2. A portion of these revenues shall be used, through or in cooperation with other international or regional organizations, to promote efficient, safe and economic exploitation of mineral resources of the seabed; to promote research on means to protect the marine environment; to advance other international efforts designed to promote safe and efficient use of the marine environment; to promote development of knowledge of the International Seabed Area; and to provide technical assistance to Contracting Parties or their nationals for these purposes, without discrimination.

ARTICLE 6
Neither this Convention nor any rights granted or exercized pursuant thereto shall affect the legal status of the superjacent waters as high seas, or that of the air space above those waters.

ARTICLE 7
All activities in the marine environment shall be conducted with reasonable regard for exploration and exploitation of the natural resources of the International Seabed Area.

ARTICLE 8
Exploration and exploitation of the natural resources of the International Seabed Area must not result in any unjustifiable interference with other activities in the marine environment.

ARTICLE 9
All activities in the International Seabed Area shall be conducted with strict and adequate safeguards for the protection of human life and safety and of the marine environment.

ARTICLE 10
All exploration and exploitation activities in the International Seabed Area shall be conducted by a Contracting Party or group of Contracting Parties or natural or juridical persons under its or their authority or sponsorship.

1. Each Contracting Party shall take appropriate measures to ensure that those conducting activities under its authority or sponsorship comply with this Convention.

2. Each Contracting Party shall make it an offense for those conducting activities under its authority or sponsorship in the International Seabed Area to violate the provisions of this Convention. Such offences shall be punishable in accordance with administrative or judicial procedures established by the Authorizing or Sponsoring Party.

3. Each Contracting Party shall be responsible for maintaining public order on manned installations and equipment operated by those authorized or sponsored by it.

4. Each Contracting Party shall be responsible for damages caused by activities which it authorizes or sponsors to any other Contracting Party or its nationals.

5. A group of States acting together, pursuant to agreement among them or through an international organization, shall be jointly and severally responsible under this Convention.

ARTICLE 12

All disputes arising out of the interpretation or application of this Convention shall be settled in accordance with provisions of Section E of Chapter IV.

CHAPTER II
GENERAL RULES

A. Mineral Resources

ARTICLE 13

1. All exploration and exploitation of the mineral deposits of the International Seabed Area shall be licensed by the International Seabed Resource Authority or the appropriate Trustee Party. All licenses shall be subject to the provisions of this Convention.

2. Detailed rules to implement this Chapter are contained in Appendices A, B and C.

ARTICLE 14

1. There shall be fees for licenses for mineral exploration and exploitation.

2. The fees referred to in paragraph 1 shall be reasonable and be

designed to defray the administrative expenses of the International
Seabed Resource Authority and of the Contracting Parties in dis-
charging their responsibilities in the International Seabed Area.

ARTICLE 15

1. An exploitation license shall specify the minerals or categories
of minerals and the precise area to which it applies. The categories
established shall be those which will best promote simultaneous and
efficient exploitation of different minerals.

2. Two or more licensees to whom licenses have been issued for
different materials in the same or overlapping areas shall not un-
justifiably interfere with each other's activities.

ARTICLE 16

The size of the area to which an exploitation license shall apply
and the duration of the license shall not exceed the limits provided
for in this Convention.

ARTICLE 17

Licensees must meet work requirements specified in this Convention as a condition of retaining an exploitation license prior to and
after commercial production is achieved.

ARTICLE 18

Licensees shall submit work plans and production plans, as well as
reports and technical data acquired under an exploitation license, to
the Trustee Party or the Sponsoring Party, as appropriate, and, to
the extent specified by this Convention, to the International Seabed
Resource Authority.

ARTICLE 19

1. Each Contracting Party shall be responsible for inspecting, at
regular intervals, the activities of licensees authorized or sponsored
by it. Inspection reports shall be submitted to the International Seabed Resource Authority.

2. The International Seabed Resource Authority, on its own initiative or at the request of any interested Contracting Party, may
inspect any licensed activity in co-operation with the Trustee Party
or Sponsoring Party, as appropriate, in order to ascertain that the
licensed operation is being conducted in accordance with this Convention. In the event the International Seabed Resource Authority
believes that a violation of this Convention has occurred, it shall

inform the Trustee Party or Sponsoring Party, as appropriate, and request that suitable action be taken. If, after a reasonable period of time, the alleged violation continues, the International Seabed Resource Authority may bring the matter before the Tribunal in accordance with Section E of Chapter IV.

ARTICLE 20

1. Licenses issued pursuant to this Convention may be revoked only for cause in accordance with the provisions of this Convention.

2. Expropriation of investments made, or unjustifiiable interference with operations conducted, pursuant to a license is prohibited.

ARTICLE 21

1. Due notice must be given, by Notices to Mariners or other recognized means of notification, of the construction or deployment of any installations or devices for the exploration or exploitation of mineral deposits, and permanent means for giving warning of their presence must be maintained. Any installations or devices extending into the superjacent waters which are abandoned or disused must be entirely removed.

2. Such installations and devices shall not possess the status of islands and shall have no territorial sea of their own.

3. Installations or devices may not be established where interference with the use of recognized sea lanes or airways is likely to occur.

B. *Living Resources of the Seabed*

ARTICLE 22

Subject to the provisions of Chapter III, each Contracting Party may explore and exploit the seabed living resources of the International Seabed Area in accordance with such conservation measures as are necessary to protect the living resources of the International Seabed Area and to maximize their growth and utilization.

C. *Protection of the Marine Environment, Life and Property*

ARTICLE 23

1. In the International Seabed Area, the International Seabed Resource Authority shall prescribe Rules and Recommended Practices, in accordance with Chapter V of this Convention, to ensure:

   a. The protection of the marine environment against pollution arising from exploration and exploitation activities such as drilling, dredging, excavation, disposal of waste, construction and operation or maintenance of installations and pipelines and other devices;

b. The prevention of injury to persons, property and marine resources arising from the aforementioned activities;

c. The prevention of any unjustifiable interference with other activities in the marine environment arising from the aforementioned activities.

2. Deep drilling in the International Seabed Area shall be undertaken only in accordance with the provisions of this Convention.

D. Scientific Research

ARTICLE 24

1. Each Contracting Party agrees to encourage, and to obviate interference with, scientific research.

2. The Contracting Parties shall promote international co-operation in scientific research concerning the International Seabed Area:

a. By participating in international programs and by encouraging co-operation in scientific research by personnel of different countries;

b. Through effective publication of research programs and the results of research through international channels;

c. By co-operation in measures to strengthen the research capabilities of developing countries, including the participation of their nationals in research programs.

E. International Marine Parks and Preserves

ARTICLE 25

In consultation with the appropriate international organizations or agencies, the International Seabed Resource Authority may designate as international marine parks and preserves specific portions of the International Seabed Area that have unusual educational, scientific or recreational value. The establishment of such a park or preserve in the International Trusteeship Area shall require the approval of the appropriate Trustee Party.

CHAPTER III
THE INTERNATIONAL TRUSTEESHIP

ARTICLE 26

1. The International Trusteeship Area is that part of the International Seabed Area comprising the continental or island margin between the boundary described in Article 1 and a line, beyond the

base of the continental slope, or beyond the base of the slope of an island situated beyond the continental slope, where the downward inclination of the surface of the seabed declines to a gradient of 1:_____.[2]

2. Each Trustee Party shall permanently delineate the precise seaward boundary of the International Trusteeship Area off its coast by straight lines not exceeding 60 nautical miles in length, following the general direction of the limit specified in paragraph 1. Such lines shall connect fixed points at the limit specified in paragraph 1, defined permanently by co-ordinates of latitude and longitude. Areas between or landward of such points may have a surface gradient of less than 1:_____.[2] Where an elongate basin or plain have a surface gradient of less than 1:_____[2] transects an area having a gradient of more than 1:_____,[2] a straight boundary line more than 60 nautical miles in length, but not exceeding the lesser of one-fourth of the length of that part of the basin transecting the area having a gradient of more than 1:_____[2] or 120 nautical miles, may be drawn across the basin or plain.

3. Each Trustee Party shall submit the description of its boundary to the International Seabed Boundary Review Commission within five years of the entry into force of this Convention for that Party. Boundaries not accepted by that Commission and not resolved by negotiation between the Commission and the Trustee Party within one year shall be submitted by the Commission to the Tribunal for adjudication in accordance with Section E of Chapter IV. (Additional consideration will be given to problems raised by enclosed and semienclosed seas.)

ARTICLE 27

1. Except as specifically provided for in this Chapter, the coastal State shall have no greater rights in the International Trusteeship Area off its coast than any other Contracting Party.

2. With respect to exploration and exploitation of the natural resources of that part of the International Trusteeship Area in which it acts as trustee for the international community, each coastal State, subject to the provisions of this Convention, shall be responsible for:

[2] The precise gradient should be determined by technical experts, taking into account, among other factors, ease of determination, the need to avoid dual administration of single mineral deposits, and the avoidance of including excessively large areas in the International Trusteeship area.

a. Issuing, suspending and revoking mineral exploration and exploitation licenses;

b. Establishing work requirements, provided that such requirements shall not be less than those specified in Appendix A;

c. Ensuring that its licensees comply with this Convention, and, if it deems it necessary, applying standards to its licensees higher than or in addition to those required under this Convention, provided such standards are promptly communicated to the International Seabed Resource Authority;

d. Supervising its licensees and their activities;

e. Exercise civil and criminal jurisdiction over its licensees, and persons acting on their behalf, while engaged in exploration or exploitation;

f. Filing reports with the International Seabed Resource Authority;

g. Collecting and transferring to the International Seabed Resource Authority all payments required by this Convention;

h. Determining the allowable catch of the living resources of the seabed and prescribing other conservation measures regarding them;

i. Enacting such laws and regulations as are necessary to perform the above functions.

3. Detailed rules to implement this Chapter are contained in Appendix C.

ARTICLE 28

In performing the functions referred to in Article 27, the Trustee Party may, in its discretion:

a. Establish the procedures for issuing licenses;

b. Decide whether a license shall be issued;

c. Decide to whom a license shall be issued, without regard to the provisions of Article 3;

d. Retain (a figure between $33\frac{1}{3}\%$ and 50% will be inserted here) of all fees and payments required by this Convention;

e. Collect and retain additional license and rental fees to defray its administrative expenses, and collect, and retain (a figure between $33\frac{1}{3}\%$ and 50% will be inserted here) of, other additional fees and payments related to the issuance or retention of a license, with annual notification to the International Seabed Resource Authority of the total amount collected;

f. Decide whether and by whom the living resources of the seabed shall be exploited, without regard to the provisions of Article 3.

The Trustee Party may enter into an agreement with the International Seabed Resource Authority under which the International Seabed Resource Authority will perform some or all of the trusteeship supervisory and administrative functions provided for in this Chapter in return for an appropriate part of the Trustee Party's share of international fees and royalties.

Where a part of the International Trusteeship Area is off the coast of two or more Contracting Parties, such Parties shall, by agreement, precisely delimit the boundary separating the areas in which they shall respectively perform their trusteeship functions and inform the International Seabed Boundary Review Commission of such delimitation. If agreement is not reached within three years after negotiations have commenced, the International Seabed Boundary Review Commission shall be requested to make recommendations to the Contracting Parties concerned regarding such delimitation. If agreement is not reached within one year after such recommendations are made, the delimitation recommended by the Commission shall take effect unless either Party, within 90 days thereafter, brings the matter before the Tribunal in accordance with Section E of Chapter IV.

CHAPTER IV

THE INTERNATIONAL SEABED RESOURCE AUTHORITY

A. General

1. The International Seabed Resource Authority is hereby established.

2. The principal organs of the Authority shall be the Assembly, the Council, and the Tribunal.

The permanent seat of the Authority shall be at _____.

Each Contracting Party shall recognize the juridical personality of the Authority. The legal capacity, privileges and immunities of the Authority shall be the same as those defined in the Convention on the Privileges and Immunities of the Specialized Agencies of the United Nations.

B.   *The Assembly*

ARTICLE 34

1. The Assembly shall be composed of all Contracting Parties.

2. The first session of the Assembly shall be convened _____. The Assembly shall thereafter be convened by the Council at least once every three years at a suitable time and place. Extraordinary sessions of the Assembly shall be convened at any time on the call of the Council, or the Secretary-General of the Authority at the request of one-fifth of the Contracting Parties.

3. At meetings of the Assembly a majority of the Contracting Parties is required to constitute a quorum.

4. In the Assembly each Contracting Party shall exercise one vote.

5. Decisions of the Assembly shall be taken by a majority of the members present and voting, except as otherwise provided in this Convention.

ARTICLE 35

The powers and duties of the Assembly shall be to:

a. Elect its President and other officers;

b. Elect the members of the Council in accordance with Article 36;

c. Determine its rules of procedure and constitute such subsidiary organs as it considers necessary or desirable;

d. Require the submission of reports from the Council;

e. Take action on any matter referred to it by the Council;

f. Approve proposed budgets for the Authority, or return them to the Council for reconsideration and resubmission;

g. Approve proposals by the Council for changes in the allocation of the net income of the Authority within the limits prescribed in Appendix D, or return them to the Council for reconsideration and resubmission;

h. Consider any matter within the scope of this Convention and make recommendations to the Council or Contracting Parties as appropriate;

i. Delegate such of its powers as it deems necessary or desirable to the Council and revoke or modify such delegation at any time;

j. Consider proposals for amendments of this Convention in accordance with Article 76.

C. The Council

ARTICLE 36

1. The Council shall be composed of twenty-four Contracting Parties and shall meet as often as necessary.

2. Members of the Council shall be designated or elected in the following categories:

   a. The six most industrially advanced Contracting Parties shall be designated in accordance with Appendix E;

   b. Eighteen additional Contracting Parties, of which at least twelve shall be developing countries, shall be elected by the Assembly, taking into account the need for equitable geographical distribution.

3. At least two of the twenty-four members of the Council shall be landlocked or shelf-locked countries.

4. Elected members of the Council shall hold office for three years following the last day of the Assembly at which they are elected and thereafter until their successors are designated or elected. Designated members of the Council shall hold office until replaced in accordance with Appendix E.

5. Representatives on the Council shall not be employees of the Authority.

ARTICLE 37

1. The Council shall elect its President for a term of three years.

2. The President of the Council may be a national of any Contracting Party, but may not serve during his term of office as its representative in the Assembly or on the Council.

3. The President shall have no vote.

4. The President shall:

   a. Convene and conduct meetings of the Council.

   b. Carry out the functions assigned to him by the Council.

ARTICLE 38

Decisions by the Council shall require approval by a majority of all its members, including a majority of members in each of the two categories referred to in paragraph 2 of Article 36.

ARTICLE 39

Any Contracting Party not represented on the Council may participate, without a vote, in the consideration by the Council or any of the subsidiary organs, of any question which is of particular interest to it.

ARTICLE 40

The powers and duties of the Council shall be to:

a. Submit annual reports to the Contracting Parties;

b. Carry out the duties specified in this Convention and any duties delegated to it by the Assembly;

c. Determine its rules of procedure;

d. Appoint and supervise the Commissions provided for in this Chapter, establish procedures for the co-ordination of their activities, and determine the terms of office of their members;

e. Establish other subsidiary organs, as may be necessary or desirable, and define their duties;

f. Appoint the Secretary-General of the Authority and establish general guidelines for the appointment of such other personnel as may be necessary;

g. Submit proposed budgets to the Assembly for its approval, and supervise their execution;

h. Submit proposals to the Assembly for changes in the allocation of the net income of the Authority within the limits prescribed in Appendix D;

i. Adopt and amend Rules and Recommended Practices in accordance with Chapter V, upon the recommendation of the Rules and Recommended Practices Commission;

j. Issue emergency orders, at the request of any Contracting Party, to prevent serious harm to the marine environment arising out of any exploration or exploitation activity and communicate them immediately to licensees, and authorizing or sponsoring Parties, as appropriate;

k. Establish a fund to provide emergency relief and assistance in the event of a disaster to the marine environment resulting from exploration or exploitation activities;

l. Establish procedures for co-ordination between the International Seabed Resource Authority, and the United Nations, its specialized agencies and other international or regional organizations concerned with the marine environment;

m. Establish or support such international or regional centers, through or in co-operation with other international and regional organizations, as may be appropriate to promote study and research of the natural resources of the seabed and to train nationals of any Contracting Party in related science and the technology of the exploration and exploitation, taking into account the special needs of developing States Parties to this Convention;

n. Authorize and approve agreements with a Trustee Party, pursuant to Article 29, under which the International Seabed Resource Authority will perform some or all of the Trustee Party's functions.

ARTICLE 41

In furtherance of Article 5, paragraph 2, of this Convention, the Council may, at the request of any Contracting Party and taking into account the special needs of developing States Parties to this Convention:

a. Provide technical assistance to any Contracting Party to further the objectives of this Convention;

b. Provide technical assistance to any Contracting Party to help it to meet its responsibilities and obligations under this Convention;

c. Assist any Contracting Party to augment its capability to derive maximum benefit from the efficient administration of the International Trusteeship Area.

D. The Commissions

ARTICLE 42

1. There shall be a Rules and Recommended Practices Commission, an Operations Commission, and an International Seabed Boundary Review Commission.

2. Each Commission shall be composed of five to nine members appointed by the Council from among persons nominated by Contracting Parties. The Council shall invite all Contracting Parties to submit nominations.

3. No two members of a Commission may be nationals of the same State.

4. A member of each Commission shall be elected its President by a majority of the members of the Commission.

5. Each Commission shall perform the functions specified in this Convention and such other functions as the Council may specify from time to time.

ARTICLE 43

1. Members of the Rules and Recommended Practices Commission shall have suitable qualifications and experience in seabed resources management, ocean sciences, maritime safety, ocean and

marine engineering, and mining and mineral technology and practices. They shall not be full-time employees of the Authority.

2. The Rules and Recommended Practices Commission shall:

a. Consider, and recommend to the Council for adoption, Annexes to this Convention in accordance with Chapter V;

b. Collect from any communicate to Contracting Parties information which the Commission considers necessary and useful in carrying out its functions.

ARTICLE 44

1. Members of the Operations Commission shall have suitable qualifications and experience in the management of seabed resources, and operation of marine installations, equipment and devices.

2. The Operations Commission shall:

a. Issue licenses for seabed mineral exploration and exploitation, except in the International Trusteeship Area;

b. Supervise the operations of licensees in co-operation with the Trustee or Sponsoring Party, as appropriate, but shall not itself engage in exploration or exploitation;

c. Perform such functions with respect to disputes between Contracting Parties as are specified in Section E of this Chapter;

d. Initiate proceedings pursuant to Section E of this Chapter for alleged violations of this Convention, including but not limited to proceedings for revocation or suspension of licenses;

e. Arrange for and review the collection of international fees and other forms of payment;

f. Arrange for the collection and dissemination of information relating to licensed operations;

g. Supervise the performance of the functions of the Authority pursuant to any agreement between a Trustee Party and the Authority under Article 29;

h. Issue deep drilling permits.

ARTICLE 45

1. Members of the International Seabed Boundary Review Commission shall have suitable qualifications and experience in marine hydrography, bathymetry, geodesy and geology. They shall not be full-time employees of the Authority.

2. The International Seabed Boundary Review Commission shall:

a. Review the delineation of boundaries submitted by Contracting Parties in accordance with Articles 1 and 26 to see that they conform to the provisions of this Convention, negotiate any differences with Contracting Parties, and if these differences are not resolved initiate proceedings before the Tribunal in accordance with Section E of this Chapter;

b. Make recommendations to the Contracting Parties in accordance with Article 30;

c. At the request of any Contracting Party, render advice on any boundary question arising under this Convention.

E. *The Tribunal*

ARTICLE 46

1. The Tribunal shall decide all disputes and advise on all questions relating to the interpretation and application of this Convention which have been submitted to it in accordance with the provisions of this Convention. In its decisions and advisory opinions the Tribunal shall also apply relevant principles of international law.

2. Subject to an authorization under Article 96 of the Charter of the United Nations, the Tribunal may request the International Court of Justice to give an advisory opinion on any question of international law.

ARTICLE 47

1. The Tribunal shall be composed of five, seven, or nine independent judges, who shall possess the qualifications required in their respective countries for appointment to the highest judicial offices, or shall be lawyers especially competent in matters within the scope of this Convention. In the Tribunal as a whole the representation of the principal legal systems of the world shall be assured.

2. No two of the members of the Tribunal may be nationals of the same State.

ARTICLE 48

1. Each Contracting Party shall be entitled to nominate candidates for membership on the Tribunal. The Council shall elect the Tribunal from a list of these nominations.

2. The members of the Tribunal shall be elected for nine years and may be reelected, provided however, that the Council may establish procedures for staggered terms. Should such procedures be established, the judges whose terms are to expire in less than nine years shall be chosen by lots drawn by the Secretary-General.

3. The members of the Tribunal shall continue to discharge their

duties until their places have been filled. Though replaced, they shall finish any cases which they may have begun.

4. A member of the Tribunal unable to perform his duties may be dismissed by the Council on the unanimous recommendation of the other members of the Tribunal.

5. In case of a vacancy, the Council shall elect a successor who shall hold office for the remainder of his predecessor's term.

ARTICLE 49

The Tribunal shall establish its rules of procedure; elect its President; appoint its Registrar and determine his duties and terms of service; and adopt regulations for the appointment of the remainder of its staff.

ARTICLE 50

1. Any Contracting Party which considers that another Contracting Party has failed to fulfil any of its obligations under this Convention may bring its complaint before the Tribunal.

2. Before a Contracting Party institutes such proceedings before the Tribunal it shall bring the matter before the Operations Commission.

3. The Operations Commission shall deliver a reasoned opinion in writing after the Contracting Parties concerned have been given the opportunity both to submit their own cases and to reply to each other's case.

4. If the Contracting Party accused of a violation does not comply with the terms of such opinion within the period laid down by the Commission, the other Party concerned may bring the matter before the Tribunal.

5. If the Commission has not given an opinion within a period of three months from the date when the matter was brought before it, either Party concerned may bring the matter before the Tribunal without waiting further for the opinion of the Commission.

ARTICLE 51

1. Whenever the Operations Commission, acting on its own initiative or at the request of any licensee, considers that a Contracting Party or a licensee has failed to fulfil any of its obligations under this Convention, it shall issue a reasoned opinion in writing on the matter after giving such party the opportunity to submit its comments.

2. If the party concerned does not comply with the terms of such opinion within the period laid down by the Commission, the latter may bring a complaint before the Tribunal.

ARTICLE 52

1. If the Tribunal finds that a Contracting Party or a licensee has failed to fulfil any of its obligations under this Convention, such party shall take the measures required for the implementation of the judgment of the Tribunal.

2. When appropriate, the Tribunal may decide that the Contracting Party or the licensee who has failed to fulfil its obligations under this Convention shall pay to the Authority a fine of not more than $1,000 for each day of the offence, or shall pay damages to the other party concerned, or both.

3. In the event the Tribunal determines that a licensee has committed a gross and persistent violation of the provisions of this Convention and has not within a reasonable time brought his operations into compliance, the Council may, as appropriate, either revoke his licence or request that the Trustee Party revoke it. The licensee shall not, however, be deprived of his licence if his actions were directed by a Trustee or Sponsoring Party.

ARTICLE 53

If disputes under Articles 1, 26 and 30 have not been resolved by the time and methods specified in those Articles, the International Seabed Boundary Review Commission shall bring the matter before the Tribunal.

ARTICLE 54

1. Any Contracting Party which questions the legality of measures taken by the Council, the Rules and Practices Commission, the Operations Commission, or the Seabed Boundary Review Commission on the grounds of a violation of this Convention, lack of jurisdiction, infringement of important procedural rules, unreasonableness, or misuse of powers, may bring the matter before the Tribunal.

2. Any person may, subject to the same conditions, bring a complaint to the Tribunal with regard to a decision directed to that person, or a decision which, although in the form of a rule or a decision directed to another person, is of direct concern to the complainant.

3. The proceedings provided for in this Article shall be instituted within a period of two months, dating, as the case may be, either

from the publication of the measure concerned or from its notification to the complainant, or, in default thereof, from the day on which the latter learned of it.

4. If the Tribunal considers the appeal well-founded, it should declare the measure concerned to be null and void, and shall decide to what extent the annulment shall have retroactive application.

ARTICLE 55

1. The organ responsible for a measure declared null and void by the Tribunal shall be required to take the necessary steps to comply with the Tribunal's judgment.

2. When appropriate, the Tribunal may require that the Authority repair or pay for any damage caused by its organs or by its officials in the performance of their duties.

ARTICLE 56

When a case pending before a court or tribunal of one of the Contracting Parties raises a question of the interpretation of this Convention or of the validity or interpretation of measures taken by an organ of the Authority, the court or tribunal concerned may request the Tribunal to give its advice thereon.

ARTICLE 57

The Tribunal shall also be competent to decide any dispute connected with the subject matter of this Convention submitted to it pursuant to an agreement, licence, or contract.

ARTICLE 58

If a Contracting Party fails to perform the obligations incumbent upon it under a judgment rendered by the Tribunal, the other Party to the case may have recourse to the Council, which shall decide upon measures to be taken to give effect to the judgment. When appropriate, the Council may decide to suspend temporarily, in whole or in part, the rights under this Convention of the Party failing to perform its obligations, without impairing the rights of licensees who have not contributed to the failure to perform such obligations. The extent of such a suspension should be related to the extent and seriousness of the violation.

ARTICLE 59

In any case in which the Council issues an order in emergency circumstances to prevent serious harm to the marine environment, any directly affected Contracting Party may request immediate review by the Tribunal, which shall promptly either confirm or suspend the application of the emergency order pending the decision of the case.

ARTICLE 60

Any organ of the International Seabed Resource Authority may request the Tribunal to give an advisory opinion on any legal question connected with the subject matter of this Convention.

F. The Secretariat

ARTICLE 61

The Secretariat shall comprise a Secretary-General and such staff as the International Seabed Resource Authority may require. The Secretary-General shall be appointed by the Council from among persons nominated by Contracting Parties. He shall serve for a term of six years, and may be reappointed.

ARTICLE 62

The Secretary-General shall:

a. Be the chief administrative officer of the International Seabed Resource Authority, and act in that capacity in all meetings of the Assembly and the Council;

b. Report to the Assembly and the Council on the work of the International Seabed Resource Authority;

c. Collect, publish and disseminate information which will contribute to mankind's knowledge of the seabed and its resources;

d. Perform such other functions as are entrusted to him by the Assembly or the Council.

ARTICLE 63

1. In the performance of their duties the Secretary-General and the staff shall not seek or receive instructions from any government or from any other external authority. They shall refrain from any action which might reflect on their position as international officials responsible only to the International Seabed Resource Authority.

2. Each Contracting Party shall respect the exclusively international character of the responsibilities of the Secretary-General and the staff and shall not seek to influence them in the discharge of their responsibilities.

ARTICLE 64

1. The staff of the International Seabed Resource Authority shall be appointed by the Secretary-General under the general guidelines established by the Council.

2. Appropriate staffs shall be assigned to the various organs of the Authority as required.

3. The paramount consideration in the employment of the staff and in the determination of the conditions of service shall be the necessity of securing the highest standards of efficiency, competence, and integrity. Due regard shall be paid to the importance of recruiting the staff on as wide a geographical basis as possible.

G. *Conflicts of Interest*

ARTICLE 65

No representative to the Assembly or the Council nor any member of the Tribunal, Commissions, subsidiary organs (other than advisory bodies or consultants), or the Secretariat, shall, while serving as such a representative or member, be actively associated with or financially interested in any of the operations of any enterprise concerned with exploration or exploitation of the natural resources of the International Seabed Area.

CHAPTER V
RULES AND RECOMMENDED PRACTICES

ARTICLE 66

1. Rules and Recommended Practices are contained in Annexes to this Convention.

2. Annexes shall be consistent with this Convention, its Appendices, and any amendments thereto. Any Contracting Party may challenge an Annex, an amendment to an Annex, or any of their provisions, on the grounds that it is unnecessary, unreasonable or constitutes a misuse of powers, by bringing the matter before the Tribunal in accordance with Article 54.

3. Annexes shall be adopted and amended in accordance with Article 67. Those Annexes adopted along with this Convention, if any, may be amended in accordance with Article 67.

ARTICLE 67

The Annexes to this Convention and amendments to such Annexes shall be adopted in accordance with the following procedure:

a. They shall be prepared by the Rules and Recommended Practices Commission and submitted to the Contracting Parties for comments;

b. After receiving the comments, the Commission shall prepare a revised text of the Annex or amendments thereto;

c. The text shall then be submitted to the Council which shall adopt it or return it to the Commission for further study;

d. If the Council adopts the text, it shall submit it to the Contracting Parties;

e. The Annex or an amendment thereto shall become effective within three months after its submission to the Contracting Parties, or at the end of such longer period of time as the Council may prescribe, unless in the meantime more than one-third of the Contracting Parties register their disapproval with the Authority;

f. The Secretary-General shall immediately notify all Contracting States of the coming into force of any Annex or amendment thereto.

ARTICLE 68

1. Annexes shall be limited to the Rules and Recommended Practices necessary to:

a. Fix the level, basis, and accounting procedures for determining international fees and other forms of payment, within the ranges specified in Appendix A;

b. Establish work requirements within the ranges specified in Appendices A and B;

c. Establish criteria for defining technical and financial competence of applicants for licenses;

d. Assure that all exploration and exploitation activities, and all deep drilling, are conducted with strict and adequate safeguards for the protection of human life and safety and of the marine environment;

e. Protect living marine organisms from damage arising from exploration and exploitation activities;

f. Prevent or reduce to acceptable limits interference arising from exploration and exploitation activities with other uses and users of the marine environment;

g. Assure safe design and construction of fixed exploration and exploitation installations and equipment;

h. Facilitate search and rescue services, including assistance to aquanauts, and the reporting of accidents;

i. Prevent unnecessary waste in the extraction of minerals from the seabed;

j. Standardize the measurement of water depth and the definition of other natural features pertinent to the determination of the precise location of International Seabed Area boundaries;

k. Prescribe the form in which Contracting Parties shall describe their boundaries and the kinds of information to be submitted in support of them;

l. Encourage uniformity in seabed mapping and charting;

m. Facilitate the management of a part of the international trusteeship area pursuant to any agreement between a Trustee Party and the Authority under Article 29;

n. Establish and prescribe conditions for the use of international marine parks and preserves;

2. Application of any Rule or Recommended Practice may be limited as to duration or geographic area, but without discrimination against any Contracting Party or licensee.

ARTICLE 69

The Contracting Parties agree to collaborate with each other and the appropriate Commission in securing the highest practicable degree of uniformity in regulations, standards, procedures and organizations in relation to the matters covered by Article 68 in order to facilitate and improve seabed resources exploration and exploitation.

ARTICLE 70

Annexes and amendments thereto shall take into account existing international agreements and, where appropriate, shall be prepared in collaboration with other competent international organizations. In particular, existing international agreements and regulations relating to safety of life at sea shall be respected.

ARTICLE 71

1. Except as otherwise provided in this Convention, the Annexes and amendments thereto adopted by the Council shall be binding on all Contracting Parties.

2. Recommended Practices shall have no binding effect.

ARTICLE 72

Any Contracting Party believing that a provision of an Annex or an amendment thereto cannot be reasonably applied because of special circumstances may seek a waiver from the Operations Commission and if such waiver is not granted within three months, it may appeal to the Tribunal within an additional period of two months.

CHAPTER VI
TRANSITION

ARTICLE 73

1. There shall be due protection for the integrity of investments made in the International Seabed Area prior to the coming into force of this Convention.

2. All authorizations by a Contracting Party to exploit the mineral resources of the International Seabed Area granted prior to July 1, 1970, shall be continued without change after the coming into force of this Convention provided that:

a. Activities pursuant to such authorizations shall, to the extent possible, be conducted in accordance with the provisions of this Convention;

b. New activities under such previous authorization which are begun after the coming into force of this Convention shall be subject to the regulatory provisions of this Convention regarding the protection of human life and safety and of the marine environment and the avoidance of unjustifiable interference with other uses of the marine environment;

c. Upon the expiration or relinquishment of such authorizations, or upon their revocation by the authorizing Party, the provisions of this Convention shall become fully applicable to any exploration or exploitation of resources remaining in the areas included in such authorizations;

d. Contracting Parties shall pay to the International Seabed Resource Authority, with respect to such authorizations, production payments provided for under this Convention.

3. A Contracting Party which has authorized exploitation of the mineral resources of the International Seabed Area on or after July 1, 1970 shall be bound, at the request of the person so authorized, either to issue new licenses under this Convention in its capacity as a Trustee Party, or to sponsor the application of the person so authorized to receive new licenses from the International Seabed Resource Authority. Such new license issued by a Trustee Party shall include the same terms and conditions as its previous authorization, provided that such license shall not be inconsistent with this Convention, and provided further that the Trustee Party shall itself be responsible for complying with increased obligations resulting

from the application of this Convention, including fees and other payments required by this Convention.

4. The provisions of paragraph 3 shall apply within one year after this Convention enters into force for the Contracting Party concerned, but in no event more than five years after the entry into force of this Convention.

5. Until converted into new licenses under paragraph 3, all authorizations issued on or after July 1, 1970, to exploit the mineral resources of the International Seabed Area shall have the same status as authorizations under paragraph 2. Five years after the entry into force of this Convention all such authorizations not converted into new licenses under paragraph 3 shall be null and void.

6. Any Contracting Party that has authorized activities within the International Seabed Area after July 1, 1970, but before this Convention has entered into force for such Party, shall compensate the licensee for any investment losses resulting from the application of this Convention.

ARTICLE 74

1. The membership of the Tribunal, the Commissions, and the Secretariat shall be maintained at a level commensurate with the tasks being performed.

2. In the period before the International Seabed Resource Authority acquires income sufficient for the payment of its administrative expenses the Authority may borrow funds for the payment of those expenses. The Contracting Parties agree to give sympathetic consideration to requests by the Authority for such loans.

CHAPTER VII
DEFINITIONS

ARTICLE 75

Unless another meaning results from the context of a particular provision, the following definitions shall apply:

1. "Convention" refers to all provisions of and amendments to this Convention, its Appendices, and its Annexes.

2. "Trustee Party" refers to the Contracting Party exercising trusteeship functions in that part of the International Trusteeship Area off its coast in accordance with Chapter III.

3. "Sponsoring Party" refers to a Contracting Party which sponsors an application for a license or permit before the International

Seabed Resource Authority. The term "sponsor" is used in this context.

4. "Authorizing Party" refers to a Contracting Party authorizing any activity in the International Seabed Area, including a Trustee Party issuing exploration or exploitation licenses. The term "authorize" is used in this context. In the case of a vessel, the term "Authorizing Party" shall be deemed to refer to the State of its nationality.

5. "Operating Party" refers to a Contracting Party which itself explores or exploits the natural resources of the International Seabed Area.

6. "Licensee" refers to a State, group of States, or natural or juridical person holding a license for exploration or exploitation of the natural resources of the International Seabed Area.

7. "Exploration" refers to any operation in the International Seabed Area which has as its principal or ultimate purpose the discovery and appraisal, or exploitation, of mineral deposits, and does not refer to scientific research. The term does not refer to similar activities when undertaken pursuant to an exploitation license.

8. "Deep drilling" refers to any form of drilling or excavation in the International Seabed Area deeper than 300 meters below the surface of the seabed.

9. "Landlocked or shelf-locked country" refers to a Contracting Party which is not a Trustee Party.

CHAPTER VIII

AMENDMENT AND WITHDRAWAL

ARTICLE 76

Any proposed amendment to this Convention or the appendices thereto which has been approved by the Council and a two-thirds vote of the Assembly shall be submitted by the Secretary-General to the Contracting Parties for ratification in accordance with their respective constitutional processes. It shall come into force when ratified by two-thirds of the Contracting Parties, including each of the six States designated pursuant to sub-paragraph 2(a) of Article 36 at the time the Council approved the amendments. Amendments shall not apply retroactively.

ARTICLE 77

1. Any Contracting Party may withdraw from this Convention by a written notification addressed to the Secretary-General. The Secre-

tary-General shall promptly inform the other Contracting Parties of any such withdrawal.

2. The withdrawal shall take effect one year from the date of the receipt by the Secretary-General of the notification.

APPENDIX A

Terms and Procedures
Applying to
All Licenses in The International Seabed Area

1. *Activities Requiring a License or a Permit*

1.1. Pursuant to Article 13 of this Convention, all exploration and exploitation operations in the International Seabed Area which have as their principal or ultimate purpose the discovery or appraisal, and exploitation, of mineral deposits shall be licensed.

1.2. There shall be two categories of licenses:

(a) A non-exclusive exploration license shall authorize geophysical and geochemical measurements, and bottom sampling, for the purposes of exploration. This license shall not be restricted as to area and shall grant no exclusive right to exploration nor any preferential right in applying for an exploitation license. It shall be valid for two years following the date of its issuance and shall be renewable for successive two-year periods.

(b) An exploitation license shall authorize exploration and exploitation of one of the groups of minerals described in section 5 in a specified area. The exploitation license shall include the exclusive right to undertake deep drilling and other forms of subsurface entry for the purpose of exploration and exploitation of minerals described in paragraphs 5.1(a) and 5.1(c). The license shall be for a limited period and shall expire at the end of fifteen years if no commercial production is achieved.

1.3. The right to undertake deep drilling for exploration or exploitation shall be granted only under an exploitation license.

1.4. Deep drilling for purposes other than exploration or exploitation of seabed minerals shall be authorized under a deep-drilling permit issued at no charge by the International Seabed Resource Authority, provided that:

(a) The application is accompanied by a statement from the Sponsoring Party certifying as to the applicant's technical competence and accepting liability for any damage that may result from such drilling;

(b) The application for such a permit is accompanied by a description of the location proposed for such holes, by seismograms and other pertinent information on the geology in the vicinity of the proposed drilling sites, and by a description of the equipment and procedures to be utilized;

(c) The proposed drilling, including the methods and equipment to be utilized, complies with the requirements of this Convention and is judged by the Authority not to pose an uncontrollable hazard to human safety, property, and the environment;

(d) The proposed drilling is either not within an area already under an exploitation license or is not objected to by the holder of such a license;

(e) The applicant agrees to make available promptly the geologic information obtained from such drilling to the Authority and the public.

2. *General License Procedures*

2.1. An Authorizing or Sponsoring Party shall certify the operator's financial and technical competence and shall require the operator to conform to the rules, provisions and procedures specified under the terms of the license.

2.2. Each Authorizing or Sponsoring Party shall formulate procedures to ensure that applications for licenses are handled expeditiously and fairly.

2.3. Any Authorizing or Sponsoring Party which considers that it is unable to exercise appropriate supervision over operators authorized or sponsored by it in accordance with this Convention shall be permitted to authorize or sponsor operators only if their operations are supervised by the International Seabed Resource Authority pursuant to an agreement between the Authorizing or Sponsoring Party and the International Seabed Resource Authority. In such event fees and rentals normally payable to the International Seabed Resource Authority will be increased appropriately to offset its supervisory costs.

3. *Exploration Licenses—Procedures*

3.1. All applications for exploration licenses and for their renewal shall be accompanied by a fee of from $500 to $1,500 as specified in an Annex and a description of the location of the general area to be investigated and the kinds of activities to be undertaken. A portion [a figure between 50% and 66⅔% will be inserted here] of the fee shall be forwarded by the Authorizing or Sponsoring Party to the Authority together with a copy of the application.

3.2. The Authorizing or Sponsoring Party shall transmit to the Authority the description referred to in paragraph 3.1 and its assurance that the activities will not be harmful to the marine environment.

3.3. The Authorizing or Sponsoring Party may require the operator to pay and may retain, an additional license fee not to exceed $3,000, to help cover the administrative expenses of that Party.

3.4. Exploration licenses shall not be renewed in the event the operator has failed to conform his activities under the prior license to the provisions of this Convention or to the conditions of the license.

4.   *Exploitation Licenses—Procedures*

4.1. All applications for exploitation licenses shall be accompanied by a fee of from $5,000 to $15,000, per block, as specified in an Annex. A portion [a figure between 50% and 66⅔% will be inserted here] of the fee shall be forwarded by the Authorizing or Sponsoring Party to the Authority together with a copy of the application.

4.2. Pursuant to section 5 below, applications shall identify the category of minerals in the specific area for which a license is sought.

4.3. When a license is granted to an applicant for more than one block at the same time, only a single certificate need be issued.

4.4. The Authorizing or Sponsoring Party may require the operator to pay, and may retain, an additional license fee not to exceed $30,000, to help cover the administrative expenses of that Party.

4.5. The license fee described in paragraph 4.1 shall satisfy the first two years' rental fee.

5.   *Exploitation Rights—Categories and Size of Blocks*

5.1. Licenses to exploit shall be limited to one of the following categories of minerals:

(a) Fluids or minerals extracted in a fluid state, such as oil, gas, helium, nitrogen, carbon dioxide, water, geothermal energy, sulfur and saline minerals.

(b) Manganese-oxide nodules and other minerals at the surface of the seabed.

(c) Other minerals, including category (b) minerals that occur beneath the surface of the seabed and metalliferous muds.

5.2. An exploitation license shall be issued for a specific area of the seabed and subsoil vertically below it, hereinafter referred to as a "block." The methods for defining the boundaries of blocks, and of portions thereof, shall be specified in an Annex.

5.3. In the category described in paragraph 5.1(a) the block shall be approximately 500 square kilometers, which shall be reduced to a quarter of a block when production begins. Each exploitation license shall apply to not more than one block, but exploitation licenses to a rectangle containing as many as 16 contiguous blocks may be taken out under a single certificate and reduced by three quarters to a number of blocks, a single block, or a portion of a single block when production begins. The relinquishment requirement shall not apply to licenses issued for areas of one quarter of a block or less.

5.4. In the category described in paragraph 5.1(b) the block shall be approximately 40,000 kilometers, which shall be reduced to a quarter of a block when production begins. Each exploitation license shall apply to not more than one block, but exploitation licenses to a rectangle containing as many as four contiguous blocks may be taken out under a single certificate and reduced to a single block, or to a portion of a single block comprising one fourth their total area, when production begins. The relinquishment requirement shall not apply to licenses issued for areas of one quarter of a block or less.

5.5. In the category described in paragraph 5.1(c) the block shall be approximately 500 square kilometers, which shall be reduced to one eighth of a block when production begins. Each license shall apply to not more than one block, but exploitation licenses to as many as 8 contiguous blocks may be taken out under a single certificate and reduced to a single block, or to a portion of a single block comprising one eighth their total area, when production begins. The relinquishment shall not apply to issued for one eighth of a block or less.

5.6. Applications for exploitation licenses may be for areas smaller than the maximum stated above.

5.7. Operators may at any time relinquish rights to all or part of the licensed area.

5.8. Commercial production shall be deemed to have commenced or to be maintained when the value at the site of minerals exploited is not less than $100,000 per annum. The required minimum and the method of ascertaining this value shall be determined by the Authority.

5.9. If the commercial production is not maintained, the exploitation license shall expire within five years of its cessation, but when production is interrupted or suspended for reasons beyond the operator's control, the duration of the license shall be extended by a time equal to the period in which production has been suspended for reasons beyond the operator's control.

6. *Rental Fees and Work Requirements*

Rental Fees

6.1. Prior to attaining commercial production the following annual rental fees shall be paid beginning in the third year after the license has been issued: (a) $2–$10 per square kilometer, as specified in an appropriate Annex, for the category of minerals described in paragraph 5.1(a); $2–$10 per 100 square kilometers for the category of minerals described in paragraph 5.1(b) of Appendix A; $2–$10 per square kilometer for the category of minerals described in paragraph 5.1(c).

6.2. The rates in paragraph 6.1 shall increase at the rate of 10% per annum, calculated on the original base rental fee, for the first ten years after the third year, and shall increase 20% per annum for the following two years, calculated on the original base rental fee.

6.3. After commercial production begins, the annual rental fee shall be $5,000–$25,000 per block, regardless of block size.

6.4. The rental fee shall be payable annually in advance to the Authorizing or Sponsoring Party which shall forward a portion [a figure between 50% and 66⅔% will be inserted here] of the fees to the Authority. The Authorizing or Sponsoring Party may require the operator to pay, and may retain, an additional rental fee, not to exceed an amount equal to the amount paid pursuant to paragraphs 6.1–6.3, to help cover the administration expenses of that Party.

Work Requirements

6.5. Prior to attaining commercial production, the operator shall deposit a work requirement fee or post a sufficient bond for that amount, for each license at the beginning of each year.

6.6. The minimum annual work requirement fee for each block shall increase in accordance with the following schedule:

Para. 5.1(a) and (c) minerals		*Para. 5.1(b) minerals*	
YEARS	AMOUNT PER ANNUM	YEARS	AMOUNT PER ANNUM
1–5	$ 20,000	1–2	$ 20,000
6–10	180,000	3–10	120,000
11–15	200,000	11–15	200,000
	$2,000,000		$2,000,000

The minimum annual work requirement for a portion of a block shall be an appropriate fraction of the above, to be specified in an Annex.

6.7. The work requirement fee shall be refunded to the operator upon receipt of proof by the Authorizing Party or Sponsoring Party that the amount equivalent to the fee has been expended in actual operations. Expenditures for on-land design or process research and equipment purchase or off-site construction cost directly related to the licensed block or group of blocks shall be considered to apply toward work requirements up to 75% of the amount required.

6.8. Expenditures in excess of the required amount for any given year shall be credited to the requirement for the subsequent year or years.

6.9. In the absence of satisfactory proof that the required expenditure has been made in accordance with the foregoing provisions of this section, the deposit will be forfeited.

6.10. If cumulative work requirement expenditures are not met at the end of the initial five-year period, the exploitation license shall be forfeited.

6.11. After commercial production begins the operator shall make an annual deposit of at least $100,000 at the beginning of each year; or shall post a sufficient bond for that amount, which shall be refunded in an amount equivalent to expenditures on or related to the block and the value of production at the site.

6.12. If production is suspended or delayed for reasons beyond the operator's control, the operator shall not be required to make the deposit or post the bond required in subparagraph 6.11.

7. *Submission of Work Plans and Data Under Exploitation Licenses Prior to Commencement of Commercial Production*

7.1. Exploitation license applications shall be accompanied by a general description of the work to be done and the equipment and methods to be used. The licensee shall submit subsequent changes in his work plan to the Sponsoring or Authorizing Party for review.

7.2. The licensee shall furnish reports at specified intervals to the Authorizing or Sponsoring Party supplying proof that he has fulfilled the specified work requirements. Copies of such reports shall be forwarded to the Authority.

7.3. The licensee shall maintain records of drill logs, geophysical data and other data acquired in the area to which his license refers, and shall provide access to them to the Authorizing or Sponsoring Party on request.

7.4. At intervals of five years, or when he relinquishes his rights to all or part of the area or when he submits a production plan as described in Section 8, the operator shall transmit to the Authorizing or Sponsoring Party such maps, seismic sections, logs, assays, or reports as are specified in an Annex to this Convention. The Authorizing or Sponsoring Party shall hold such data in confidence for ten years after receipt, but shall make the data available on request to the Authority for its confidential use in the inspection of operations.

7.5. The data referred to in paragraph 7.4 shall be transmitted to the Authority ten years after receipt by the Authorizing or Sponsoring Party, and made available by the Authority for public inspection. Such data shall be transmitted to the Authority immediately upon revocation of a license.

8. *Production Plan and Producing Operations*

8.1. Prior to beginning commercial production the licensee shall submit a production plan to the Authorizing or Sponsoring Party and through such Party to the Authority.

8.2. The Authorizing or Sponsoring Party and the Authority shall require such modifications in the plan as may be necessary for it to meet the requirements of this Convention.

8.3. Any change in the licensee's production plan shall be submitted to the Authorizing or Sponsoring Party and through such Party to the Authority for their review and approval.

8.4. Not later than three months after the end of each year from the issuance of the license the licensee shall transmit to the Authorizing or Sponsoring Party for forwarding to the Authority production reports and such other data as may be specified in an Annex to this Convention.

8.5. The operator shall maintain geologic, geophysical and engineering records and shall provide access to them to the Authorizing or Sponsoring Party on its request. In addition, the operator shall submit annually such maps, sections, and summary reports as are specified in Annexes to this Convention.

8.6. The Sponsoring or Authorizing Party shall hold such maps and reports in confidence for ten years from the time received but shall make them available on request to the Authority for its confidential use in the inspection of operations.

8.7. Such maps and reports shall be transmitted to the Authority and shall be made available by it for public inspection not later than ten years after receipt by the Sponsoring or Authorizing Party.

9. *Unit Operations*

9.1. Accumulations of fluids and other minerals that can be made to migrate from one block to another and that would be most rationally mined by an operation under the control of a single operator but that lie astride the boundary of adjacent blocks licensed to different operators shall be brought into unit management and production.

9.2. With respect to deposits lying astride the seaward boundary of the International Trusteeship Area, the Operations Commission shall assure unit management and production, giving the Trustee and Sponsoring Parties and their licensees a reasonable time to reach agreement on an operation plan.

10. *Payments on Production*

10.1. When commercial production begins under an exploitation license, the operator shall pay a cash production bonus of $500,000 to $2,000,000 per block, as specified in an Annex to this Convention, to the Authorizing or Sponsoring Party.

10.2. Thereafter, the operator shall make payments to the Authorizing or Sponsoring Party which are proportional to production, in the nature of total payments ordinarily made to governments under similar conditions. Such payments shall be equivalent to 5 to 40 per cent of the gross value at the site of oil and gas, and 2 to 20 per cent of the gross value at the site of other minerals, as specified in an Annex to this Convention. The total annual payment shall not be less than the annual rental fee under paragraph 6.3.

10.3. The Sponsoring Party shall forward all payments under this section to the Authority. The Authorizing Party shall forward a portion [a figure between 50% and 66⅔% will be inserted here] of such payments to the Authority.

11. *Graduation of Payments According to Environment and Other Factors*

11.1. The levels of payments and work requirements, as well as the rates at which such payments and work requirements escalate over time, may be graduated to take account of probable risk and cost to the investor, including such factors as water depth, climate, volume of production, proximity to existing production, or other factors affecting the economic rent that can reasonably be anticipated from mineral production in a given area.

11.2. Any graduated levels and rates shall be described and categorized in an Annex in such a way as to affect all licensees in each category equally and not to discriminate against or favor individual Parties or groups of Parties, or their nationals.

11.3. Any increases in such levels of payments or requirements shall apply only to new licenses or renewals and not to those already in force.

12. *Liability*

12.1. The operator and his Authorizing or Sponsoring Party, as appropriate, shall be liable for damage to other users of the marine environment and for clean-up and restoration costs of damage to the land environment.

12.2. The Authorizing or Sponsoring Party, as appropriate, shall require operators to subscribe to an insurance plan or provide other means of guaranteeing responsibility, adequate to cover the liability described in paragraph ———.

(*Note:* More detailed provisions on liability should be included.)

13. *Revocation*

13.1. In the event of revocation pursuant to Article 52 of this Convention, there shall be no reimbursement for any expense incurred by the licensee prior to the revocation. The licensee shall, however, have the right to recover installations or equipment within six months of the date of the revocation of his license. Any installations or devices not removed by that time shall be removed and disposed of by the Authority, or the Authorizing or Sponsoring Party, at the expense of the licensee.

14. *International Fees and Payments*

14.1. The Authority shall specify the intervals at which fees and other payments collected by an Authorizing or Sponsoring Party shall be transmitted.

14.2. No Contracting Party shall impose or collect any tax, direct or indirect, on fees and other payments to the Authority.

14.3. All fees and payments required under this Convention shall be those in force at the time a license was issued or renewed.

14.4. All fees and payments to the Authority shall be transmitted in convertible currency.

APPENDIX B
Terms and Procedures Applying to
Licenses in the International Seabed Area beyond
the International Trusteeship Area

1. *Entities Entitled to Obtain Licenses*

   1.1. Contracting Parties or a group of Contracting Parties, one of which shall act as the operating or sponsoring Party for purposes of fixing operational or supervisory responsibility, are authorized to apply for and obtain exploration and exploitation licenses. Any Contracting Party or group of Contracting Parties, which applies for a license to engage directly in exploration or exploitation, shall designate a specific agency to act as operator on its behalf for the purposes of this Convention.

   1.2. Natural or juridical persons are authorized to apply for and obtain exploration and exploitation licenses from the International Seabed Resource Authority if they are sponsored by a Contracting Party.

2. *Exploration Licenses—Procedures*

   2.1. Licenses shall be issued promptly by the Authority through the Sponsoring Party to applicants meeting the requirements specified in Appendix A.

3. *Exploitation Licenses—Procedures*

   3.1. The Sponsoring Party shall certify as to the technical and financial competence of the operator, and shall transmit the operator's work plan.

   3.2. An application for an exploitation license shall be preceded by a notice of intent to apply for a license submitted by the operator to the Authority and the prospective Sponsoring Party. Such a notice of intent, when accompanied by evidence of the deposit of the license fee referred to in paragraph 4.1 of Appendix A, shall reserve the block for one hundred and eighty days. Notices of intent may not be renewed.

   3.3. Notices of intent shall be submitted sealed to the Authority and opened at monthly intervals at previously announced times.

   3.4. Subject to the compliance with these procedures, if only one notice of intent has been received for a particular block, the applicant shall be granted a license, except as provided in paragraphs 3.6–3.8.

3.5. If more than one notice of intent to apply for a license for the same block or portion thereof is received at the same opening, the Authority shall notify the applicants and their Sponsoring Parties that the exploitation license to the block or portion thereof will be sold to the highest bidder at a sale to be held one hundred and eighty days later, under the following terms:

(a) The bidding shall be on a cash bonus basis and the minimum bid shall be twice the license fee;

(b) Bids shall be sealed;

(c) The bidding shall be limited to such of the original applicants whose applications have been received in the interim from their sponsoring Parties;

(d) Bids shall be announced publicly by the Authority when they are opened. In the event of a tie, the tie bidders shall submit a second sealed bid to be opened 28 days later;

(e) The final award shall be announced publicly by the Authority within seven days after the bids have been opened.

3.6. In the event of the termination, forfeiture, or revocation of an exploitation license to a block, or relinquishment of a part of a block, the block or portion thereof will be offered for sale by sealed competitive bidding on a cash bonus basis in addition to the current license fee. The following provisions shall apply to such a sale:

(a) The availability of such a block, or portion thereof, for bidding shall be publicly announced by the Authority as soon as possible after it becomes available, and a sale following the above procedures shall be held within one hundred and eighty days after a request for an exploitation license on the block has been received;

(b) The bidding shall be open to all sponsored operators, including, except in the case of revocation, the operator who previously held the exploitation license to the block or to the available portion thereof.

(c) If the winning bid is submitted by an operator who previously held the exploitation right to the same block, or to the same portion thereof, the work requirement will begin at the level that would have applied if the operator had continuously held the block.

3.7. Blocks, or portions thereof, contiguous to a block on which production has begun shall also be sold by sealed competitive bidding under the terms specified in paragraph 3.6.

3.8. Blocks, or separate portions thereof, from which hydrocarbons or other fluids are being drained, or are believed to be drained, by production from another block shall be offered for sale by sealed competitive bidding under the terms specified in paragraph 3.7, at the initiative of the Authority.

3.9. Geologic and other data concerning blocks or portions thereof open for bidding pursuant to paragraphs 3.6–3.8 which are no longer confidential shall be made available to the public prior to the bidding date. Data on blocks, or separate portions thereof, for which the license has been revoked for violations shall be made available to the public within 30 days after revocation.

3.10. Exploitation licenses shall only be transferable with the approval of the Sponsoring Party and the Authority, provided that the transferee meets the requirements of this Convention, is sponsored by a Contracting Party, and a transfer fee is paid to the Authority in the amount of $250,000. This fee shall not apply in transfers between parts of the same operating enterprise.

4. *Duration of Exploitation Licenses*

4.1. If commercial production has been achieved within fifteen years after the license has been issued, the exploitation license shall be extended automatically for twenty additional years from the date commercial production has commenced.

4.2. At the completion of the twenty-year production period referred to in paragraph 4.1, the operator with the approval of the Sponsoring Party shall have the option to renew his license for another twenty years at the rental fees and payment rates in effect at the time of renewal.

4.3. At the end of the forty-year term, or earlier if the license is voluntarily relinquished or expires, pursuant to paragraph 5.9 of Appendix A, the block or blocks, or separate portions of blocks, to which the license applied shall be offered for sale by competitive bidding on a cash bonus basis. The previous licensee shall have no preferential right to such block, or separate portion thereof.

5. *Work Requirements*

   5.1. The annual work requirement fee per block shall be specified in an Annex in accordance with the following schedule:

Para. 5.1(a) and (c) minerals			*Para. 5.1(b) minerals*		
YEARS	AMOUNT PER	ANNUM	YEARS	AMOUNT PER	ANNUM
1–5	$ 20,000–	60,000	1–2	$ 20,000–	60,000
6–10	180,000–	540,000	3–10	120,000–	360,000
11–15	200,000–	600,000	11–15	200,000–	600,000
Total	$2,000,000–6,000,000		Total	$2,000,000–6,000,000	

The minimum annual work requirement for a portion of a block shall be an appropriate fraction of the above, to be specified in an Annex.

   5.2. Work expenditures with respect to one or more blocks may be considered as meeting the aggregate work requirements on a group of blocks originally licensed in the same year, to the same operator, in the same category, provided that the number of such blocks shall not exceed sixteen in the case of category 5.1(a) of Appendix A, four in the case of category 5.1(b) and eight in the case of category 5.1(c).

   5.3. Should the aggregate work requirement expenditure of $2,000,000 to $6,000,000 be spent prior to the end of the thirteenth year, an additional work requirement of $25,000–$50,000 as specified in an Annex, shall be met until commercial production begins or until the expiration of the fifteen-year period.

   5.4. After commercial production begins the operator shall at the beginning of each year, deposit $100,000 to $200,000 as specified in an Annex, or with the Sponsoring Party post a bond for that amount. Such deposit or bond shall be returned in an amount equivalent to expenditures on or related to the block and the value of production at the site. A portion [a figure between 50% and 66⅔% will be inserted here] of any funds not returned shall be transmitted to the Authority.

6. *Unit Management*

   The Operations Commission shall assure unit management and production pursuant to Section 9 of Appendix A, giving the licensees and their Sponsoring Parties a reasonable time to reach agreement on a plan for unit operation.

APPENDIX C
Terms and Procedures for Licenses in
the International Trusteeship Area

1. *General*

    1.1. Unless otherwise specified in this Convention, all provisions of this Convention except those in Appendix B shall apply to the International Trusteeship Area.

2. *Entities Entitled to Obtain Licenses*

    2.1. The Trustee Party, pursuant to Chapter III, shall have the exclusive right, in its discretion, to approve or disapprove applications for exploration and exploitation licenses.

3. *Exploration and Exploitation Licenses*

    3.1 The Trustee Party may use any system for issuing and allocating exploration and exploitation licenses.

    3.2. Copies of licenses issued shall be forwarded to the Authority.

4. *Categories and Size of Blocks*

    4.1. The Trustee Party may license separately one or more related minerals of the categories listed in paragraph 5.1 of Appendix A.

    4.2. The Trustee Party may establish the size of the block for which exploitation licenses are issued within the maximum limits specified in Appendix A.

5. *Duration of Exploitation Licenses*

    5.1. The Trustee Party may establish the term of the exploitation license and the conditions if any, under which it may be renewed, provided that its continuance after the first 15 years is contingent upon the achievement of commercial production.

6. *Work Requirements*

    6.1. The Trustee Party may set the work requirements at or above those specified in Appendix A and put these in terms of work to be done rather than funds to be expended.

7. *United Management*

    7.1. When a deposit most rationally extracted under unit management lies wholly within the International Trusteeship Area, or astride its landward boundary, the Trustee Party concerned shall assure unit management and production pursuant to Section 9.1 of Appendix A, and shall submit the plan for unit operation to the Operations Commission.

7.2. With respect to deposits lying astride a boundary between two Trustee Parties in the International Trusteeship Area, such Parties shall agree on a plan to assure unit management and production, and shall submit the operation plan to the Operations Commission.

8. *Proration*

8.1. The Trustee Party may establish proration, to the extent permitted by its domestic law.

9. *Payments*

9.1. Pursuant to sub-paragraph (e) of Article 28, the Trustee Party may collect fees and payments related to the issuance or retention of a license in addition to those specified in this Convention, including but not limited to payments on production higher than those required by this Convention.

9.2. The Trustee Party shall transfer to the Authority a portion (a figure between 50% and 66⅔% will be inserted here) of the fees and payments referred to in paragraph 9.1 except as otherwise provided in paragraphs 3.3, 4.4 and 6.4 of Appendix A.

(NOTE: Further study is required on the means to assure equitable application of the principle contained in paragraph 9.2 to socialist and nonsocialist parties and their operations.)

10. *Standards*

10.1. The Trustee Party may impose higher operating, conservation, pollution and safety standards than those established by the Authority, and may impose additional sanctions in case of violations of applicable standards.

11. *Revocation*

11.1. The Trustee Party may suspend or revoke licenses for violation of this Convention, or of the rules it has established pursuant thereto, or in accordance with the terms of the license.

APPENDIX D
Division of Revenue

1. *Disbursements*

    1.1. All disbursements shall be made out of the net income of the Authority, except as otherwise provided in paragraph 2 of Article 74.

2. *Administrative Expenses of the International Seabed Resource Authority*

    2.1. The Council, in submitting the proposed budget to the Assembly shall specify what proportion of the revenues of the Authority shall be used for the payment of the administrative expenses of the Authority.

    2.2. Upon approval of the budget by the Assembly, the Secretary-General is authorized to use the sums allotted in the budget for the expenses specified therein.

3. *Distribution of the Net Income of the Authority*

    3.1. The net income, after administrative expenses, of the Authority shall be used to promote the economic advancement of developing States Parties to this Convention and for the purposes specified in paragraph 2 of Article 5, and in other Articles of this Convention.

    3.2. The portion to be devoted to economic advancement of developing States Parties to this Convention shall be divided among the following international development organizations as follows:

    (NOTE: A list of international and regional development organizations should be included here, indicating percentages assigned to each organization.)

    3.3. The Council shall submit to the Assembly proposals for the allocation of the income of the Authority within the limits prescribed by this Appendix.

    3.4. Upon approval of the allocation by the Assembly, the Secretary-General is authorized to distribute the funds.

APPENDIX E
Designated Members of the Council

1. Those six Contracting Parties which are both developed States and have the highest gross national product shall be considered as the six most industrially advanced Contracting Parties.

2. The six most industrially advanced Contracting Parties at the time of the entry into force of this Convention shall be deemed to be: _____
They shall hold office until replaced in accordance with this Appendix.

3. The Council, prior to every regular session of the Assembly, shall decide which are the six most industrially advanced Contracting Parties. It shall make rules to ensure that all questions relating to the determination of such Contracting Parties are considered by an impartial committee before being decided by the Council.

4. The Council shall report its decision to the Assembly, together with the recommendations of the impartial committee.

5. Any replacements of the designed members of the Council shall take effect on the day following the last day of the Assembly to which such a report is made.